The Rutgers
Picture Book

This volume has been published with the
cooperation and support of the Rutgers University Libraries
and the Class of 1940.

by Michael Moffatt

with a foreword by Richard P. McCormick

Richard P. McCormick, Editorial Consultant
Richard W. Mitchell, Graphics Consultant

The Rutgers Picture Book

An Illustrated History of Student Life in the Changing College and University

Rutgers University Press, New Brunswick, New Jersey

Book design by Gerda Spirig

Library of Congress Cataloging in Publication Data

Moffatt, Michael, 1944–
    The Rutgers picture book.

    1. Rutgers University—Students—Pictorial
works.   I. Title.
LD4756.M63   1985   378.749′42   84–24953
ISBN 0–8135–1091–0
ISBN 0–8135–1092–9

Table of Contents

Foreword

Here is a "picture book" that will be something more than a coffee table ornament. For those who identify with Rutgers, past and present, but also for a wider audience intrigued by changes in the culture of academic youth over time, *The Rutgers Picture Book* will be a visual and intellectual treat.

The author, Michael Moffatt, is a gifted young anthropologist with a sensitive understanding of college students in this and previous generations. He has chosen quite deliberately to focus on the students' perceptions of Rutgers and the distinctive modes of student behavior manifested in different eras. In words and images, he depicts what might be termed "Rutgers from the bottom up."

His is not an institutional approach, featuring governing bodies, faculties, budgets, and policies, but rather an anthropological view, attuned to the manners and customs of those who came to Rutgers to study, play, protest, socialize, mature, and discover themselves. Moffatt does not engage in puffery. His endeavor has not been to glorify his subject but to take it seriously. This does not imply that his findings are in any sense dull or derogatory; on the contrary, they are fascinating and even inspiring.

It will be clear that there has always existed a creative tension between the academic institution, as represented by its authority figures, and the youths who comprise the student body. In all eras, students have managed to "do their thing," often to the dismay of their elders but usually in a way that in retrospect commands our respect, if not our full approval. They have never been content to be passive recipients of knowledge and traditional values; they have always been prone to experiment, rebel, and invent—and to insist on defending some form of autonomy. This is Moffatt's message.

In another vein, this volume gives us a kaleidoscopic view of a special universe to which we feel strong emotional ties. Those of us who shared the joys—and the trials—of student life at Rutgers can revel in the recollection of our undergraduate years and relate our experiences to the generations that preceded and followed us. We can also permit ourselves a glow of pride as we follow the uneven development of Rutgers from a small, often struggling, college in the nineteenth century to one of America's major universities today.

Richard P. McCormick
University Professor of History and
University Historian, *Emeritus*

The Rutgers Picture Book is an illustrated history of Rutgers College and University from its founding in 1766 to the present, with an emphasis on student perspectives. Student perspectives are embodied in visual materials—in photographs, drawings, and other graphics—but they are also conceptual—ways of looking at the institution at different times in its more than two centuries of history. Historical photographs in particular often seem to speak for themselves, to show directly how things really were. But in fact most of the photos collected here, like virtually all old photos, are highly stylized—examples of photographic genres closely connected to very particular conceptions. In the text, and especially in the captions of this volume, an effort has been made to suggest what some of these ideas have been—of Rutgers in particular, of college life and college youth more generally—as projected in photographs and in other illustrations that have come down to us.

Preface

Officially, Rutgers has seen itself in a variety of ways since its colonial founding—as a "literary institution"; as a "scientific school" interested in producing useful citizens; as an Ivy League–like liberal arts college; as a "men's college" and a "women's college"; and as a large, complex, pragmatic state university. Though the history of these official views is sketched here, the focus of this volume is different: Rutgers from the students' point of view. Students have never seen the college and university in the same way as have the "authorities" (faculty, administrators, alumni, trustees, and parents); for over two hundred years they have led their own quasi-independent lives in the school, emphasizing their own distinctive concerns and organizing themselves in their own ways. Through the years, the students have changed as radically as the institution itself: from the earnest, respectable pre–Civil War "literary" students to the college diehards of the late nineteenth century, to the activists and careerists of the modern era.

The student point of view is emphasized here for two reasons. First, it is the most pervasive—the perspective shared by the vast majority of those who have been connected with Rutgers over the years, even when many have gone on to more mature affiliations and their perspectives have changed. And second, it has been institutionally important in often unappreciated ways. Like American college students elsewhere, Rutgers students have often been a step ahead of the official institution. As will be suggested below, the student literary societies of the early nineteenth century anticipated the late-nineteenth-century curricular changes: the late-nineteenth-century student extracurriculum was taken over by the college in the early twentieth century. And much more recently, student-initiated changes from the 1960s—in minority education and coeducation—are still with us in the 1980s.

The Rutgers Picture Book is based on the rich material in the Rutgers University Libraries' Special Collections and Archives: photos, illustrations, original documents, the "biographical files" of the alumni, student publications such as the *Scarlet Letter*, student diaries and scrapbooks, and many others. This book was originally conceived by Hendrik Edelman, University Librarian, as a way of presenting archival material on Rutgers history. The Class of 1940 made a generous contribution toward its expenses, and Rutgers University Press agreed to collaborate on an equal basis with the library in the complex production of the volume. Richard P. McCormick, University Historian, suggested the focus on students and was willing to serve as editorial consultant. In what follows, I have relied extensively on Professor McCormick's excellent institutional history, *Rutgers: A Bicentennial History* (1966), a far more comprehensive book than the present volume. Anyone whose interest in Rutgers history is whetted by *The Rutgers Picture Book* should go on to *Rutgers: A Bicentennial History*. My other main scholarly inspirations have been Rutgers historian John Gillis's fascinating work on the history of youth, and New York University historian James McLachlan's splendid studies of nineteenth-century American higher education (see "Sources and Further Reading"). I have done anthropological research of my own on current student life at Rutgers—"participant observation" while living in several Rutgers dormitories—and historical research on nineteenth-century Rutgers students.

Thanks to Ruth J. Simmons, University Archivist and Head of Special Collections and Archives, for making research facilities available for an intensive summer of work on this project; and to Susan E. Avallone, Patricia Buickerood, Edward Skipworth, Albert C. King, Ronald Becker, Ferenc Varga, and Maxine Lurie, also in Special Collections and Archives, for their help (and thanks to Ms. Avallone for a few personal photos). My thanks as well to Richard W. Mitchell for his photographic expertise; to David Burns '70, Assistant Vice-President for Student Life Policy and Services, for proofreading, ethnography, and the suicide anecdote mentioned in Chapter 2; to Jean Sidar, Vice President and Secretary of the University, for scholarly and editorial advice and details on George H. Cook; to Parker Worley, Director of the Rutgers-Camden Library, and Clement Price, Professor of History, Rutgers-Newark, for consultation on the scanty non–New Brunswick archival material; to Barbara M. Smith at *Rutgers Alumni Magazine* for interest and help; to *Rutgers Alumni Magazine*, the *Rutgers News Service*, *Targum*, and *The Rutgers Review* for supplying some excellent contemporary photos; to Robert E. Smith, director, Rutgers Sports Information, for making available equally fine recent sports pictures; to Dr. Tod Marder, Professor of Art History, for chatting with me about Rutgers architecture; to the Rutgers Alumni-Faculty Club for the painting of the original football game; to Mary Hartman, Dean of Douglass College, for her histories of the Douglass Sacred Path ceremony and the Hall-Mills case; to Howard Crosby, former Dean of Students at Rutgers College, for his reminiscences; to Stayton Wood, current Dean of Students at Rutgers College, for his interest and encouragement; to Ed Lipman '33, Rutgers Trustee, Bill Gillam '40, and Carl Woodward, Jr., '40, for more reminiscences (thanks also to Messrs. Gillam and Woodward for the use of a few personal photos); to Louis Miller '87 for a page from his scrapbook; to Martin Goldman for the photo of Stayton Wood; to Renata Miller '84 for her editorial eye; and to my son, Alan Dalsass, for help with the manuscript.

The Rutgers
Picture Book

S.E. View of Rutgers Colle[ge]

PLAN
of the CITY of
NEW-BRUNSWICK
from actual SURVEY.
Published by
A.A. MARCELUS & TERHUNE & LETSON
New-Brunswick 1829

"The Pleasures of Student Life" 1766–1864

What could modern Rutgers have in common with the college founded in New Brunswick, New Jersey, over two hundred years ago by the Dutch Reformed Church in America? Modern Rutgers is a secular, coeducational institution with over 40,000 students, 2,500 faculty members, 7 campuses, and a large administrative bureaucracy. The early college was an incomparably smaller, poorer, simpler men's school attached to a church. Even the name has changed. It was Queen's College for the first sixty years of the college's existence. But there are some broad continuities, continuities characteristic of American education in general, not just of Rutgers. Like modern college education, early Rutgers education was not intrinsically vocational; Rutgers graduates were not usually ready to enter the work world, but went on to apprenticeships in business, law, or medicine, or to other schools, including theological seminaries—such as, but not necessarily, the Reformed Church Seminary in New Brunswick (the Grammar School and Rutgers were founded at the same time, while the Seminary dates from 1784). College was an extension of youth, a time to grow up and get ready for adult life, much as it is today, though the English idea of a sequestered "campus" did not take hold at Rutgers until the late nineteenth century.

Nor was Rutgers strictly a religious college. Many non–Reformed Church students attended from its earliest days, and the college was as dedicated to providing a "useful" education as it was to insuring the piety of its graduates (which it did worry about in ways long since forgotten). Early American colleges were founded by particular denominations not only to insure an American supply of clergy; they were also intended to educate and "civilize" the general population. This was the church's role because no other institution was capable of undertaking it in eighteenth-century America; only the churches possessed—in their clergy—a reliable stock of educated men qualified to be college faculty members.

Rutgers was the eighth college founded in the American colonies, under a charter from Governor William Franklin in 1766. Even among the small, poor colleges of its day, it was particularly tiny and weak. Its parent church, the Dutch Reformed Church, had one of the smallest denominations in the colonies, and the faction that founded and supported Rutgers in its early years was a minority within this church. Rutgers was located in New Brunswick, New Jersey, because its founding faction was concentrated in the Raritan River valley. But the fact that most of the Dutch constituency was located further north in New Jersey and in southern and central New York (together with the fact that another Dutch institution—Union College—was founded in 1795 in Schenectady, New York) created enrollment problems for the college throughout its first century.

Thus in 1774 the college consisted of twenty male students (the college education of females was undreamed of until Oberlin inaugurated it in the 1830s) and two tutors meeting in a converted tavern—The Sign of the Red Lion—on Albany and Neilson streets (now part of the new Johnson & Johnson world-headquarters site). During the American Revolution, New Brunswick was occupied by British

◄
NEW BRUNSWICK MAP, 1829
In 1829 New Brunswick had a population of less than 10,000. It was a prosperous trading town at the highest point on the Raritan River to which oceangoing vessels could easily ascend. New Brunswick took particular pride in its "literary institution," Rutgers College ("F" on this map), which had been relocated on the outskirts of the town in 1811, apparently with plenty of room to expand.

forces, and the school was relocated fifteen miles up the Raritan River to near Branchburg. One of the first tutors, John Taylor, led Revolutionary troops in many local battles, while intermittently keeping up his teaching duties; several early alumni rose rapidly in the politics of the Continental Congress. Queen's College returned to New Brunswick after the war, but the school was so impoverished that it had no graduates in the mid-1780s. In 1795, after rejecting a proposal to merge with Princeton, the college quietly expired.

In 1807 the institution was resuscitated and soon located in the building now called Old Queen's, the first building erected on the present College Avenue Campus. In 1817 the school again expired, but revived once more in 1825, thanks in part to its ownership of a valuable New Jersey state lottery. At this time it was renamed Rutgers after Henry Rutgers, a New York–based magnate who responded by giving the college the interest on a $5,000 bond and a bell. It also entered into a much closer, more controlling covenant with the synod of the Dutch church. Since 1825 Rutgers has been in continuous existence. In the 1830s it had about seventy-five students taught by three faculty members, and it did not grow much until the late 1850s.

The early college was church founded and church controlled, but it was neither exclusively Dutch nor exclusively clerical. Students with Dutch surnames were in the minority after the 1840s (though most of the non-Dutch students continued to come from the old Dutch zone), and Presbyterians, Episcopalians, Methodists, and Baptists were common in the early classes. About 40 percent of the pre–Civil War graduates went on to the clergy. Most of the rest went into the same occupations as their fathers, the classical professions of a largely rural society—law and medicine—and business. Perhaps a quarter of the pre–Civil War alumni had started out as poor boys, however, the sons of small farmers and shopkeepers or of recent immigrants to the United States. As it is today, early Rutgers was often a vehicle to a higher social class, and the accomplishments of some of the nineteenth-century alumni were impressive. Four were governors of New Jersey, for example, one was Secretary of State, one was a United States Supreme Court justice, and one, Garret A. Hobart '63, was vice-president under McKinley—and would most likely have become president had he not died before McKinley's assassination and been replaced by Teddy Roosevelt.

Compared to today's university, the early-nineteenth-century college was not only much smaller, it was also very simple organizationally. Prior to the twentieth century, Rutgers had no administration per se. The president was only *primus inter pares* among the faculty, and the sole nonteaching employee of the school before the 1880s was the janitor, an interesting figure who led the Commencement parade and provided an occasional strong arm, at faculty request, over difficult students. The faculty members were the only resident authorities in the college; they met in committee of the whole twice a week and handled everything connected with the college collectively—policy initiatives to the trustees, scheduling, registration and grading, student discipline, and instructions to the janitor. The college was too poor to afford real dormitories until 1890, so students lived either in boardinghouses downtown or with their own families in New Brunswick or in neighboring towns. The commuting student is nothing new at Rutgers; through much of the nineteenth century, one-quarter to one-third of the students lived at home.

What was it like to be a student at Rutgers before the Civil War? The curriculum sounds tough by modern standards: heavy doses of Greek and Latin, a good deal of Christian piety, some history and geography, and increasing amounts of math, science, and modern languages. The pre–Civil War years were also the classical period of in loco parentis, when the faculty clergymen were strict and comprehensive authorities over the students. They demanded punctilious respect and called recalcitrant students before their meetings on a regular basis, where they lectured and "admonished" them for their failings. The faculty informed the parents that they "consider[ed] themselves charged with the moral and religious, as well as the intellectual, training of the students" (1841 catalog), and claimed that they handed the students over in their off-hours to the close supervision of respectable families.

Appearances can be deceiving, however. The curriculum was not so deadly as it might seem to a modern student. Classical-language training was commonly regarded as the mark of wisdom, and many students were eager to acquire it. "I begin to believe," the student Andrew Hageman wrote to a hometown friend in 1847, "that there is in the Greek language a surpassing symmetry, beauty and fullness." Some students enjoyed "moral philosophy," a predecessor to the modern social sciences; it was taught to seniors by the president and was generally made relevant to their concerns in life. Many of the students liked the sciences, especially (after the 1840s) the chemistry lab, with its satisfying smells and explosions. The faculty members were not all stuffed shirts: they often knew the students well, they sometimes joked with them, and they put up with a certain amount of manipulation and disorder in the classroom. And there is evidence that early Rutgers was not very difficult academically. A student spoof from 1859 suggests that the Greek qualifying exam was a farce, that almost anyone who showed up with a smattering of the language could be admitted—for the college needed all the students it could get. In the 1880s, President Gates took pride in the fact that he had raised admissions standards to the point where one-quarter of the applicants were turned down.

As for in loco parentis—well, it also had its limits. The early student code looks tough on paper, with such strictures as "No student shall frequent taverns, or any houses of ill-repute, or be guilty of cursing, screaming, or any unbecoming language" (1787 code). But given the lack of dorms, this was easier said than enforced. Many of the boardinghouses were in fact casually supervised collections of half-a-dozen or more comradely young men, perhaps run by a widowed woman and her daughters. A student parody refers to one as "Mrs. Donley's 'Dog-Meat Hall,'" and the flavor of another is suggested in a later reminiscence about Mansion House on Albany Street, run in the 1860s by Justice James S. Nevius:

The students were so frequently brought before the judge that they thought it would be more convenient for all hands if as many as possible boarded in the house, so they applied in numbers . . . they were inclined to be somewhat noisy . . . [so they] were given the rooms in the second story of the extension, which became the famous 'Texas.' (Targum, 1895)

In 1868 the faculty voted to enlist the help of Justice Nevius to discover who had "exploded" the campus "back building" (the latrine) one evening; but the judge got nowhere with the problem.

Some of what early-nineteenth-century Rutgers students did with their free time reminds us of modern students. There were easygoing sorts like Garret Schenck, who, according to his diary, spent one fairly typical two-week period in 1851: studying in a desultory fashion five times, calling on young ladies six times, visiting with male friends twenty times, going to bars twice, and staying out all night once. Schenck was not mentioned in the disciplinary notes of the faculty during this time. And there were busy sorts like William Griffis, who clattered around the landscape on trains doing assorted church business. Before the rise of athleticism in the late nineteenth century, sports were simple, unorganized affairs, and early-nineteenth-century students—like the faculty—believed that a brisk evening constitutional would clear the system of the impurities that the sedentary scholar's life built up. Early-nineteenth-century students were also fond of music and singing—folk songs known to everyone, not the college songs of the late nineteenth century.

Other extracurricular activities were unique to student life in the early nineteenth century—especially that part of college life of which the students were fondest: their "literary societies." The student literary society was a remarkable institution found in virtually every early American college—one that is particularly hard to see as precisely extracurricular in the modern sense of the term. For in the literary societies, the students gave themselves the education that the early college did not. The college did not teach them English composition; in the literary societies, older students gave writing lessons to younger students. The college did not give them the oratorical practice essential for future preachers, lawyers, and politicians; in the literary societies, weekly "declamations" and debates were conducted. The college library was open one hour a week, and contained mostly classical and religious volumes; in the literary societies, there were large, accessible collections of more current books: philosophy, history, politics, economy, and lots of novels. The literary societies resembled the later fraternities in being nominally secret. But virtually everyone belonged to one of the two—whose relations to one another resembled those of political parties—and the faculty, alumni, and trustees thoroughly supported them, for they were aware of the education that went on inside them. Prior to the academic reforms later in the century, when most of the classical curriculum was dropped and much of what was learned in the literary societies became part of formal higher education, there simply seemed to be a different sort of division of labor: the faculty was charged with classical and moral education, the students with their intellectual self-education.

In the late 1820s Rutgers enrolled only two college classes: juniors and seniors. By the 1830s there were three and a half college classes. Most students entered in their sophomore year; only a few came in, remedially, as freshmen. First-year college students were also generally younger than today; a youth educated in classical languages and basic mathematics by a tutor at home or in a private academy could enter as young as thirteen years old. The age spread was also wider, however; poorer boys would often support themselves for a few years before coming to college and would enter in their twenties. The Dutch Reformed Church made a little money available to support preclerical students, and a number of young men worked their way through Rutgers teaching school, tutoring, or (in one case) janitoring.

Students were expected to be in chapel within fifteen minutes of the morning bell, which rang at 8:30. (A favorite student prank at Rutgers, as at other schools, was to steal the clapper to the college bell; if the bell could not ring, then the students could not be summoned out of their dispersed lodgings to their tasks.) They then had three hours of classes, one hour to a professor—lectures and "recitations," when they had to repeat back memorized material or translate portions of language texts. Classes were held six days a week, and students boarding in New Brunswick could not leave town during term without faculty permission. On Sundays they were required to attend college chapel in the morning and a New Brunswick church in the afternoon. They appear to have done so willingly. On one busy Sunday, Garret Schenck attended morning chapel and two afternoon and evening church services (commenting seriously in his diary on the sermons at each)—escorting a different young lady home from each of the church services. For three or four years, they attended all their classes with the same small set of peers; there were no electives in the Rutgers curriculum until almost the end of the century.

Through most of the nineteenth century, the academic year started in October and ended in early June. Commencement, or graduation, occurred in late June and was a big affair, with invited guests and much of the town showing up. The literary societies competed intensely with one another for honors; at Commencement, four senior honors men orated at length (as did most of the rest of the class more briefly)—and at the prestigious Junior Exhibition just before Commencement, junior orators also performed. A Commencement tradition was the appearance of broadsides called burlesques, which made fun of the entire proceedings: the faculty and alumni, the seniors, the procession from the college to the Dutch Reformed church downtown, and the speeches and music. These were perpetrated by the junior class—licensed disrespect generally ignored by the faculty (unless too scurrilous).

In their diaries and letters, pre–Civil War students talked amiably about the "pleasures of student life." Most college-age youths at the time were still under close parental authority or in apprenticeships to other adult authorities. Compared to their situations, it was not at all unpleasant to be a lightly burdened student living on one's own, surrounded by kindred spirits. But though they enjoyed college life, these pre–Civil War students had no particular loyalty to Rutgers; *college spirit* was an unknown term. Alumni loyalty was also a problem at the time, for it was invested more in the literary societies than in the college, with predictable consequences for the endowment. In the late 1840s the alumni came up with the money for the second instructional building, Van Nest Hall, partly because they thought the societies were threatened by the new fraternities. Van Nest provided quarters for the two literary societies—and for new scientific equipment.

The advent of the first of the new "secret societies," Delta Phi, founded in 1845, signaled real changes in the college from the student point of view. For Delta Phi and the second fraternity, Zeta Psi (founded 1848), proved far more impervious to faculty control than had the older literary societies. In the 1830s, a Rutgers literary society had attempted to legislate in its constitution against student "tale-bearers" ("faculty spies"), but the faculty and trustees had successfully cracked down and forbidden the prohibition. The new fraternities were seen as distinctly more secretive and subversive than the literary societies and were promptly outlawed. In this case, however, faculty suppression did not work—beginning the more assertive style of student life that developed later in the century. The fraternities' underground existence was an open secret in the college throughout the 1850s. Delta Phi was defended by a few faculty admirers as a genuinely outstanding set of young men—and in terms of their academic records and their later accomplishments, they seem to have been. Members of Zeta Psi, on the other hand, were an earthier lot who pulled off much of the campus mischief in the next fifteen years. They were involved in the first filching of the clapper to the college bell, for example. Faculty investigation never succeeded against the fraternities, which added to their early prestige among the students.

In the late 1850s Rutgers students changed in a number of ways, as did students at other colleges. More students began coming to college directly after secondary school; young men in a given class were more likely to be the same age, with the same life experiences as continual students (fewer of them had taken time out in the work world). And more students began entering in their freshman years, so that the undergraduate population was increasingly divided into four full-size college classes. In 1858 college classes first started giving themselves mottos, and a few years later the first class yearbooks were adopted—collections of the newly available wet-plate photographs and autographs. In 1859 the students founded their first real newspaper, the *Rutgers College Quarterly*. Unlike the earlier short-lived *Rutgers Literary Miscellany*, it was specifically about Rutgers college and about student concerns—it was intended to "express the free and easy side of student life" and to lobby on matters of student interest (initially, against evening chapel, for a more practical curriculum, and for college songs). In 1859 the *Quarterly* was almost closed down for publishing a particularly, disrespectful (and, 125 years later, informative) parody of the college. The irreverence of the spoof was remarkable; for example, it characterized the president of the college as a sanctimonious bore, who "gives us too much religion . . . a little, once in a while, like garlic in soup, will do very well . . . but to have everything soaked in it . . . makes us hate it." The author was thrown out and became a successful journalist in New York. The *Quarterly* survived until 1861, when the drop in enrollment brought about by the Civil War apparently finished it off.

Rutgers as an institution also began to change in the 1850s. The trustees became concerned about institutional deficiencies and thoroughly shook up the faculty, leaving only George H. Cook, science professor and assistant state geologist, with his job. In 1856 the Seminary built Hertzog Hall, on "Holy Hill," and moved out of Old Queen's. Pre–Civil War college authorities were convinced that dormitories were a bad idea, but Rutgers trustees were willing to take a chance on future clergymen; Hertzog Hall provided rooms for twenty-five preclerical undergraduates. Board was not provided, however, and the facility was not really on the "campus"; the first major dorm would not appear for thirty-three more years. By 1862, on the eve of the Civil War, Rutgers' enrollment had risen to 124, thanks mostly to the changing demography of the 1850s. The faculty numbered six, and there were three buildings on the neatly landscaped "campus" (the word was just coming into use) that is presently bounded by Somerset, College, Hamilton, and George: Old Queen's, Van Nest, and the old President's House (the present site of the parking lot next to Kirkpatrick Chapel). Rutgers was holding its own, but it showed no particular promise of ever being anything but a small, denominational college.

▶
NEW BRUNSWICK, 1845
In 1845 the new canal and railway were changing New Brunswick into a manufacturing center (the canal provided water power for factories). In this pencil copy of a lithograph viewing the city from what is now the Highland Park side of the river, the new railroad bridge leads the eye toward a bucolic town set in a pastoral landscape. Gentry sport in the foreground, and the college sits prominently on the high ground to the right. This civic booster's image of the town contrasts with a disgruntled Rutgers student's description of it in the 1870s: "the obnoxious red mud, all on end and knee deep; the beastly hotel accommodations; the narrow, puddle-stricken streets; the shanties, one story stores and consumptive vegetation" (*Scarlet Letter*, 1878).

◀
QUEEN'S, 1807
The third site of Queen's College, 1791–1809, before the college's removal to the building now called Old Queen's. Near the present intersection of George Street and Livingston Avenue; later a school for poor children.

OLD QUEEN'S
As the original building on the present campus, and the current offices of the president of the university, Old Queen's is the most photographed and sketched edifice in the iconography of Rutgers.

▶
Old Queen's in 1906, on the occasion of the inauguration of President Demarest. The students totaled around 250 at the time, and most of them are in the picture. The younger boys in the foreground are probably "rats" from the Grammar School.

▲
In the first three decades of the nineteenth century, Old Queen's was the all-purpose institutional building, housing the preparatory school (the "Grammar School"), the college, the Theological Seminary, and even providing space for a few faculty apartments. In 1830 the first subdivision occurred: Johnston Hall (still standing) was built on the corner of College Avenue and Somerset Street, to be used by the preparatory school and the student literary societies, which were moved to Van Nest Hall in 1847. This is the oldest surviving representation of Old Queen's, a drawing done prior to the addition of a cupola about 1826. The landscaping and the picket fence around the wider grounds seen in the 1847 lithograph (p. 12) were added around 1840. The front and sides are done in dressed fieldstone, while the back is unfinished—the original planners never expected the college to expand beyond this quadrant of land. The architect of Old Queen's was James McComb, who also designed New York City Hall. With its low-pitched roof and simple classical outlines, Old Queen's is a fine example of Federalist architecture and was recently designated a National Monument.

▶
A recent photograph of Old Queen's taken for a 1980 "viewbook" published by the university, in direct imitation of the 1906 photo above.

▲
RUTGERS, 1847

The much-reprinted 1847 lithograph of the college, like that of the town (pp. 8–9) is a lush, idealized, booster's view of its subject, though many of its details are accurate. The saplings on the curb side of the sidewalk in the foreground, for example, and the rest of the vegetation can be seen in later lithographs and photographs to have grown. The figures on the walk in the left center wear the medieval scholars' gowns mentioned as students' daily dress in accounts of life in the early college. The gowns were just going out of fashion at this time and were revived as graduation dress in the early twentieth century. The figures in the horse-drawn barouche are A. Bruyn Hasbrouck—the president of Rutgers from 1840–1849—and his wife.

▲
VAN NEST HALL, 1860

Van Nest Hall was the second instructional building at Rutgers, built in 1847 to house a science lab, a museum, and the literary societies. It was built in a spare and pleasing Renaissance revival style; the third story added later destroyed its lines (as well as the widow's walk shown here). Early film could not show sky tones and resulted in a washed-out effect—probably as unrealistically desolate as the 1847 lithograph (above) was unrealistically lush. To imagine the real look of the college in the mid-nineteenth century, one must split the difference between the two images.

Painted By

▼
COLLEGE, LATE 1850s
A third image of the mid-nineteenth-century college, a watercolor by T. Sandford Doolittle '59, later Professor of Rhetoric, Logic, and Mental Philosophy at Rutgers and acting President (died 1893). Probably done in the late 1850s. Despite the picture's Mediterranean sky, it has realistic aspects not found in the 1847 lithograph. It gives a sense of the neighborhood and of the unpaved streets, and it shows the campus outbuildings between Old Queen's and the President's House—the latrines that the students loved to blow up regularly as a prank. Right of the President's House on a hill in the background is Hertzog Hall, completed in 1856.

T Sandford Doolittle

Rutgers College

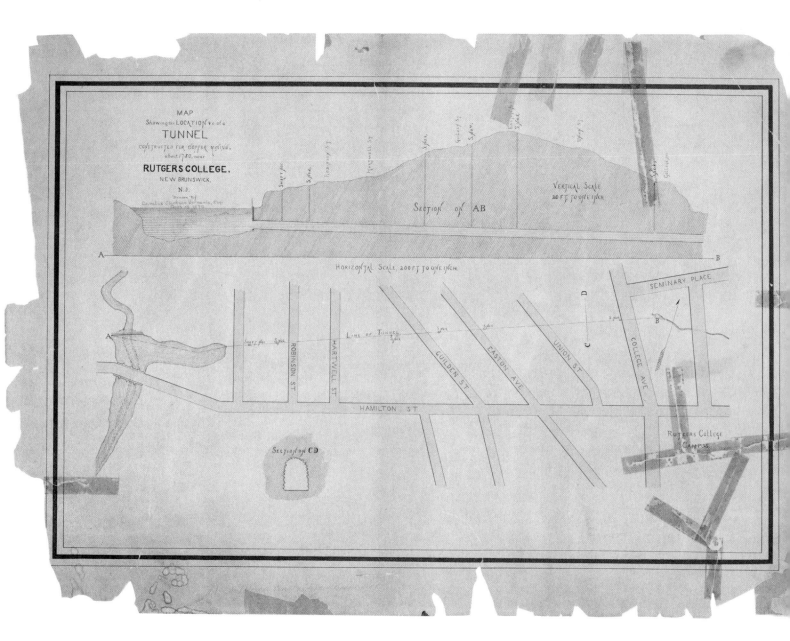

▲
THE MINE, 1750
Mine Street, off College Avenue, was named for
the drainage tunnel of a copper mine dug around
1750. The "mine" came out in a brook near the
present location of Ford Hall, and drained into
the Raritan River. Cornelius Vermeule, who drew
this map, was a graduate of the Rutgers Scientific School in 1878, and thereafter was an engi-
neer for the New Jersey geological survey.

▶
PHILIP MILLEDOLER
One of the earliest photographic images of a
Rutgers president, probably taken in the 1840s,
was a daguerreotype of Philip Milledoler, president of Rutgers, 1825–1840. The fierce look of
many faces in early daguerreotypes is due to the
long exposures. Milledoler doesn't look so bad in
comparison.

THEODORE FRELINGHUYSEN
Theodore Frelinghuysen, president of Rutgers,
1850–1862, in two different representations.

◀
Frelinghuysen in the idealized portraiture of the
mid-nineteenth century.

◀
Frelinghuysen in an early wet-plate photograph.
The stern expression is not solely due to the
exposure time, for wet-plate photography had
reduced exposures to a few seconds. Early photographs were daunting because of their ten-
dency to show unalterable human reality. Later,
retouching and other aspects of the portrait
photographer's art made photos as stylized as
paintings.

CHARTER

OF A

COLLEGE

To be erected in

NEW-JERSEY,

By the Name of

QUEEN'S-COLLEGE,

For the Education of the Youth of the said Province and the Neighbouring Colonies in true Religion and useful Learning, and particularly for providing an able and learned Protestant Ministry, according to the Constitution of the Reformed Churches in the United Provinces, using the Discipline approved and instituted by the national Synod of Dort, in the Years 1618, and 1619.

NEW-YORK,
Printed by JOHN HOLT; at the EXCHANGE,
M,DCC,LXX.

THE CHARTER, 1770
The title page of the second charter of Queen's College, 1770. Like other early American colleges, Rutgers was established both to train clergy and to provide general education ("useful learning"). Governor William Franklin, son of Benjamin Franklin, granted this charter and the previous 1766 charter (now lost).

RUTGERS DIPLOMA, 1828
The entire faculty signed Theodore Hardenbergh's diploma in 1828: Philip Milledoler, president; James Spencer Cannon, who taught metaphysics in the college and also taught in the Seminary (and was affectionately called "Old Gun" by the students); and Theodore Strong, who taught mathematics, geography, and natural philosophy. Twelve Hardenberghs graduated from Rutgers before 1916; Theodore went on to become a medical doctor.

PRÆ
Colleg
I
Legibus
Ad quos Præs
Notum sit quod
qui per Tempus legitimum apud
Studiis gnaviter Incubuit, Omni
AD GRADUM
Omnia jura immunitates et priv
Cujus rei Sigillum commune n
scripta Testimonio sunt
Curatores.
Cornelius L. Hardenbergh
Carolus Smith

ET CURATORES

Rutgersensis

...VA CÆSAREA

...eipublicæ Constituti

...us ET SINGULIS

Literæ pervenerint Salutem.

...rus Hardenbergh, Optimæ Spei Juvenem

...oratus, Probe vitam instituit, Literis et Liberalium Artium

...rcitia per Leges hujusce Academiæ postulata Sedulo Præstitit

...CALAUREI IN ARTIBUS

...ROVEXIMUS EIQUE.

...d istum gradum pertinentia Dedimus et Concessimus.

...sce Literis affixum nostraque et Professorum nomina sub-

...Nov-Brunopoli, Idibus Juliis, Anno Domini 1828.

Professores.

Wm Milledoler Præs.

Jacobus J. Cannon Metaph: Prof:

Theodorus Strong Math. et Nat. Phi. Professor.

Petr. Maverick sculp. et sculp. N.York 1830.

Monday. March 10th 1845. Faculty met. All present. The President mentioned that Mr Berdan of the Junior class had again been guilty of irregularity in his attendance at College and neglect of his duty, & that he had called a meeting for the purpose of taking his case into consideration. Mr Berdan was accordingly sent for & while waiting for his attendance the rolls were read and examined but nothing required special attention but the case of Mr Berdan. The Janitor having been unable to find Mr Berdan the faculty adjourned till tomorrow at 12½ o'clock

Wm H. Crosby.
Secy

Tuesday March 11th 1845 Faculty met. All present except Prof. Hodenpyl and Prof. Proudfit. Mr Berdan appeared before the faculty. The President reprimanded him very severely for his misconduct in staying away from College, in keeping bad company and in neglecting his studies. He confessed that he had been doing wrong, that he was sorry for it, and promised immediate amendment. He was then requested to withdraw for a few moments, when the faculty, after mature deliberation, determined to give him another trial, but at the same time, directed the Secretary to write to his father and inform him of the facts in regard to his son. Mr Berdan was then informed of the determination of the faculty, and, after another promise of amendment, he withdrew.

Wm H. Crosby.

◀
FACULTY MINUTES, 1845
A sample of the nineteenth-century faculty minutes, from 1845. The faculty met twice a week and conducted all the business of the college. The faculty of the period tried to exercise comprehensive parental authority over the students, monitoring both their on-campus and off-campus behavior. Though these minutes suggest close supervision, the faculty did not really know what the students were up to much of the time.

LITERARY SOCIETY DOCUMENTS
The minutes and other papers of the nineteenth-century student literary societies at Rutgers—Peithessophian and Philoclean—fill twenty-nine storage boxes in the Rutgers library. They are a remarkable testament, particularly through the 1850s, to the self-educational enthusiasm of the students and to their literacy.

CATALOGUE

OF THE

PEITHESSOPHIAN SOCIETY,

RUTGERS COLLEGE,

NEW BRUNSWICK, N.J.

INSTITUTED, A.D., 1825.

NEW-YORK:
JOHN H. F. BRINKERHOFF & CO.,
No. 103 FULTON-STREET.
1851.

◀
A catalog of the members of "Peitho," 1851. As fervently as did later fraternities, classes, and alumni associations, the early literary societies kept track of their present and graduate members. Due in part to limitations of printing, there is virtually no illustrative art in early-nineteenth-century student publications—in strong contrast to late-nineteenth-century student publications. Early-nineteenth-century publications also rarely mentioned such parochial matters as student life or Rutgers College itself.

Novels.

Names of Books	By whom Presented
1 "Years of the West	C. C. Hoglandy
2 209 days on the Continent	I. C Parker —
3 Guy Mannering	" " "
4 "Heart of Mid Lothian	G A Thoom
5 Prairie	I T. Demerest
6 Posthumus Papers	R H. Pruyn
7 Bravo	Chas Mc Eye
8 Alhambra	Purchased
9 Arther Clenning	Ed. T. Lyon
10 Paul Clifford	A. Lott
11 Almacks revisited	R H Pruyn
12 No Fiction	G W. Brown
13 Clara Gazue	A. Patterson
14 "Visit to London	E. S Van Arsdale
15 "Wild Irish Girl. 2 cop. 2 vol y/1	Gosman Jr. y Laing
16 Pirate	
17 Last of the Mohigans	A. C. Ludlow —
18 "Keps of the Washington Lodge —	C. A. Bogart
19 Abbot	——

◄
Novels were slightly suspect literature among respectable, churchgoing, early-nineteenth-century Americans. Thus, the student literary societies, rather than the college library, stocked them. The literary society libraries also represented disproportionately biography, modern history, and other subjects now part of the standard college curriculum. A page from the "Philo" catalog, 1830s.

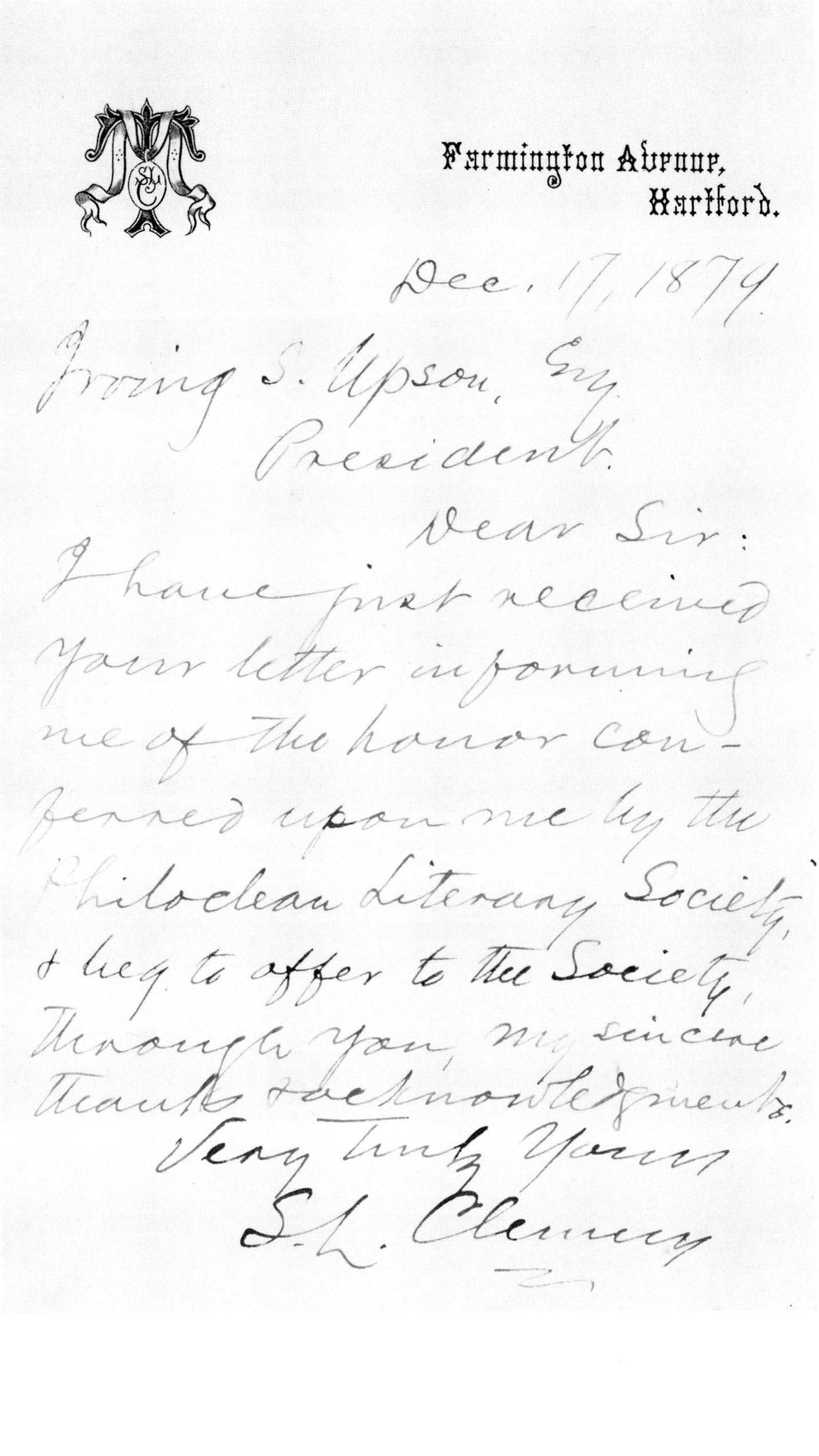

Farmington Avenue,
Hartford.

Dec. 17, 1879

Irving S. Upson, Esq.
President.

Dear Sir:

I have just received your letter informing me of the honor conferred upon me by the Philoclean Literary Society, & beg to offer to the Society, through you, my sincere thanks & acknowledgments.

Very truly Yours
S. L. Clemens

◄
A letter to the Philoclean Society from Samuel Clemens (Mark Twain) in 1879, accepting honorary membership in the society but apparently sending no money. The student president of the society at the time, Irving S. Upson, went on to be the first college bureaucrat: clerk, librarian, secretary to the faculty, registrar, and treasurer at various times in his useful service to the school.

▼
COMMENCEMENT AND BURLESQUE, 1854
Commencement was the leading college ceremony in the nineteenth century, and began with a procession from the college to the First Reformed Church, where local and regional notables joined in the festivities. Over half of the senior class spoke in the 1854 Commencement.

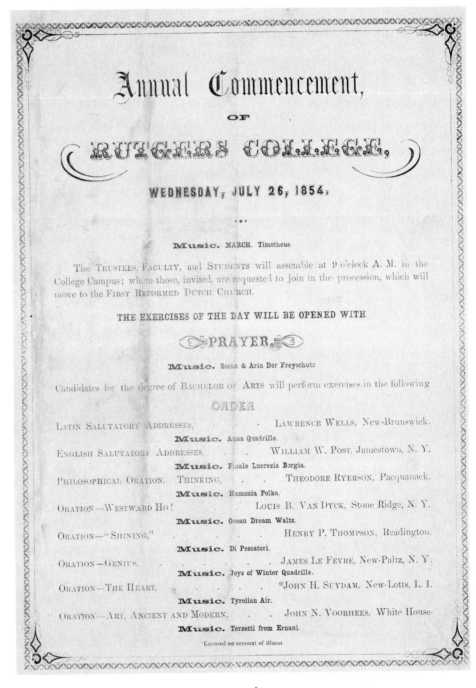

▼
Detail of the junior class burlesque of the 1854 Commencement program. Burlesques mocked the procession, the oratory, the faculty, and especially each of the senior speakers (the subject of this detail; compare names to those in the official program opposite). The worst gibes were reserved for suspected "faculty spies" and "bootlickers"—students considered disloyal to their peers. Elsewhere the burlesque also spoofed the antifraternity policies of the college in the 1850s. The current *Mugrat*, the annual parody edition of the *Targum*, is a direct descendant of the burlesque.

EXHIBITION.

Music—*French Hornpipe by Charley.*

1. LARRY (W)HELLS, Skunk Paradise,—   Latin Concoction.

" A country fop, with boots that lace,
So varnished they reflect his face.
As thus equipped he moved genteel,
A pup ran barking at his heels.
A stranger there, inquired,
' What makes the puppy bark ?'
A lad replied, of mind acute,
' He sees a puppy in the boot.'"

Music—" *The bard I quote from does not sing amiss.*"

2. BILLY SET-ERECT TIMBER, Hell-Gate,—
The Art of British Salutation.

" We grant that if he had much wit,
He was very shy of using it,
As being loth to wear it out;
And therefore bore it not about,
Unless on holidays, or so,
As men their best apparel do."

Music—" *Rogue's March.*"

3. DOUGH-HEAD WRY-ERSON, Five Points,—
Advantage of Informing.

" O, unexpected stroke, worse than of death !
Must I thus lose thee," O, my *honor*.

Music—" *I go in for Irish ladies.*"

4. LOUIS BUCK DYKE.—Rocky Mountains,—
The Giant's Grave.

" Why was I raised the meteor of the world,
Hung in the skies, and blazing as I travell'd,
Till all my fires were spent; and then cast downward ;"
To be cut out by Ryerson.

Music—*Psalm by the College Choir.*"

5. ONE-EYED THOMPSON, Reading-done,— .... Bootlicking.

" A little knowledge is a dangerous thing."

Music—*Stupidity Quadrille.*

6. LeFEVRE, New-Paltz.

This foo-foo with feverish anxiety will discourse to Prex upon " the man-
ifest propriety, and even absolute importance of grading the graduating

▼
RUTGERS COLLEGE QUARTERLY
The *Rutgers College Quarterly* was a student publication founded in 1858, midway in character between the older literary society publications and the *Targum*, founded in 1867. Like the earlier documents, it carried essays, poetry, and fiction; like the latter, it had begun to comment on student life and to articulate a distinctive student point of view within the college. The graphics were still limited.

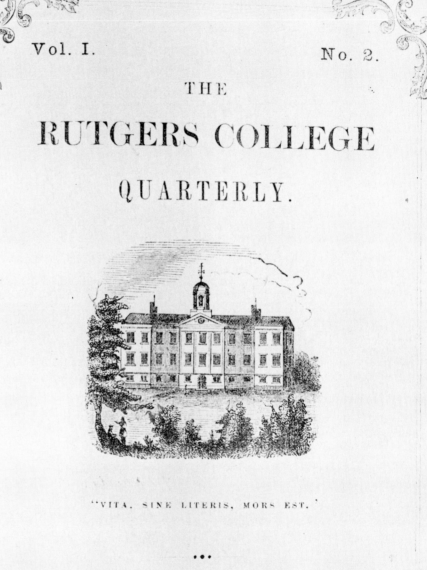

▲
FREDERICK BORDINE THOMSON
Most images of pre–Civil War Rutgers students are photographs or paintings done much later in life. One exception is this lithograph, in the romantic style of the early nineteenth century, of Frederick Bordine Thomson '31. Thomson became a clergyman and a missionary to Borneo, part of the vigorous nineteenth-century missionary tradition of the Dutch Reformed Church.

▼
EPITAPH, 1845

The death rate among nineteenth-century college students was higher than today's. Tuberculosis was a particular killer; its cure was developed by Selman Waksman '15, Nobel Prize—winner, 1952. The cause of Randolph's death is not known, but he was evidently run-down after a tough senior year. Randolph was typical of many antebellum graduates: young men, as young as thirteen years old, who had their classical training at home could enter Rutgers as sophomores. Randolph was also one of the outstanding students who founded Delta Phi. This text is from an 1886 *Targum*.

> IN
> MEMORY OF
> SAMUEL F. RANDOLPH, A. B.,
> WHO DEPARTED THIS LIFE
> AUGUST 28, 1845,
> IN THE SIXTEENTH YEAR OF HIS AGE,
> AND
> FIVE WEEKS AFTER HIS
> VALEDICTORY
> AT RUTGERS COLLEGE.
>
> 'Twas his own genius gave the fatal blow,
> And helped to plant the wound that laid him low.

▼
CLASS OF 1859

A pre—Civil War class, possibly 1859, posing in front of Van Nest Hall, in one of the earliest wet-plate photos in the Rutgers collection. Compared to late-nineteenth-century and early-twentieth-century students, there is nothing specifically collegiate, or even particularly youthful, about their dress; they could be any non-working-class young men of the period. Not until the 1870s and 1880s did college students begin to distinguish themselves strongly from other youths and mark the differences in their clothing.

Classbook, 1860
In 1859 the first "classbooks" appeared—
autograph albums. In 1860 the senior class
added the popular new photographs to them,
which unlike the older daguerreotypes could be
easily duplicated (in 1865 there were five professional photographers in New Brunswick).
Edward Janeway was one of eleven men with
that surname to graduate from Rutgers before
1916. He was later an eminent professor of medicine and a hospital administrator. His inscription
to Richard DeWitt, later a clergyman, is evidence
of the development of school spirit and class
spirit that was occurring among students at this
time.

Friend DeWitt

    How often in after life will memory recall
the days we spent in Alma Mater. We will
then think of our struggle with Greek and Latin
roots, of the odors and fumes of Prof. Cooks
gases, of parley vous francaise or it may be of
the campus with its carpet of grass on which
we have many a time reposed. But do not
forget altogether your friend and classmate
             E G Janeway
             New Brunswick
Natus Aug 31st   N.J.
    1841.

▲
HOWARD CROSBY, 1860
Howard Crosby, professor of Greek at Rutgers, 1860. Crosby was Henry Rutgers' nephew and ward, and the great-granduncle of Howard Crosby '41, assistant to the dean of students, assistant dean, and dean of students, 1941–1983.

Two changes occurred in the early 1860s that set Rutgers on a new path. The first was the appointment in 1862 of the president whom Richard P. McCormick rates the "first effective head" of Rutgers, William H. Campbell—who quickly increased the endowment. The second was the successful campaign led by George Cook, and by the mathematics professor David Murray, to have Rutgers designated New Jersey's land-grant institution. The designation was received in 1864. The other competitor was Princeton, and it was a close decision; Cook's practical knowledge of the state gained as assistant state geologist was crucial to the decision.

Rutgers went into a period of expansion, adding the Scientific School and three new buildings around Old Queen's, and increasing enrollment by the 1870s. Land-grant status was a mixed blessing, however, for New Jersey was singularly unwilling to support public education in the nineteenth century. New Jersey was the second to last state in the country, for instance, to eliminate fees in its public high schools. Rutgers bought the College Farm in 1866, founded the Agricultural Experiment Station in 1880, and built New Jersey Hall with state help in 1888. But for most of the late nineteenth century, Rutgers had to fall back on its identity as a private college. And this remained as weak a base as it had been in the early nineteenth century; enrollments fluctuated from 143 students in 1879 to 251 in 1893 to 182 in 1895. After the first decade of the twentieth century, Rutgers made some progress in its relation to the state and began to grow, ten or twenty years after other leading American state and private colleges had expanded. By 1916, the year of Rutgers' 150th anniversary, it had 537 students taught by 76 faculty members.

Twenty-five Rutgers students joined 58 alumni in fighting the Civil War (16 were killed), and a few veterans came back to Rutgers after the war; but otherwise, aside from depressing enrollments to a low of 64 in 1863, the war had little impact on Rutgers student life. Through the 1860s, the students continued to construct a new collegiate consciousness, one like that developing at Princeton, Harvard, and elsewhere. In retrospect, it was the first truly distinctive, self-aware youth culture in American society, an aggressively adolescent way of life based on college spirit, class spirit, intercollegiate sports, fraternities, and anti-intellectual values. In their increasing juvenility, late-nineteenth-century Rutgers students contrasted strongly with early-nineteenth-century students, but not in their self-direction and autonomy. Throughout the century, the significant forms of student life were almost always created entirely by students and controlled by students. In the 1880s Rutgers authorities attempted to put the students under more effective control, but their real success did not start until after 1900, when the new deans and other authorities in the expanding administration began to adapt the institution, that late-nineteenth-century students had developed, to different ends.

For the students, the 1860s and 1870s were a time of particular excitement and productivity. They revived their newspaper as the monthly *Targum* in 1869 and started the yearbook, the *Scarlet Letter*, in 1871. Scarlet had been adopted informally by the students as the Rutgers color in 1869; they had wanted it to be orange

"I'd Die for Dear Old Rutgers" 1864–1916

◀
NEW BRUNSWICK MAP, 1866
Compared to the 1829 map in Chapter 1 (p. xii), this map shows that the town has started to spread around the college grounds. The Seminary is now separately located in Hertzog Hall on "Holy Hill." The future sites of what in the first half of the twentieth century were called the Neilson Campus and the Bishop Campus are still private estates. James Neilson graduated from Rutgers in 1866 and also donated "Wood Lawn" and much additional land to what is now Douglass College.

(as in the Dutch prince of Orange), but they could not find an orange flag on the market and had to make do with scarlet. When the college got around to adopting the color officially at the end of the century, scarlet was found to have become symbolically appropriate over the thirty-odd years: the prince of Orange did not use the color orange in his family arms, it was discovered, but red. Alternatively, it was argued, scarlet could be made by mixing certain shades of red and orange.

Fraternities and college classes continued to replace the literary societies in student affections. There were seven fraternities by 1879, though the first houses were not built until the late 1880s. College classes inaugurated the "cane rush," hazing, the "cremation," and the Sophomore Exhibition in the 1860s. In the cane rush, the sophomores attacked the incoming freshmen and tried to take away their marks of adult status—their canes. Hazing was the notorious practice by which upperclassmen ganged up on obnoxious lowerclassmen, usually at night, and humiliated them in various ways. The cremation was a colorful ceremony in which the sophomores carried their least-favorite book in a mock funeral procession, and burned it—apparently a ritual attack on the rigidity of the mandatory curriculum. The Sophomore Exhibition was originally modeled on the Junior Exhibition and was held around Washington's Birthday. It soon became a rowdy event, however, with the freshmen "raking" (burlesquing) the sophomores; it was suppressed in the 1880s. Later in the century, the students added new activities and organizations to their way of life: the Glee Club, class and school plays, class dances, class banquets, class cheers, and the very exclusive class honorary societies.

Like college youths elsewhere, late-nineteenth-century Rutgers students increasingly saw themselves as an elite, and their new collegiate institutions—including distinctive language and dress—reinforced their sense of privilege. Town-and-gown disturbances increased in the late nineteenth century, and the *Targum* both made fun of "New Jerseyisms" in local dialect and remonstrated students who treated local women with less respect than they did the more acceptable women they intended to court and marry.

Athleticism also developed in the 1860s, part of the British-inspired cult of manliness that began to sweep American colleges at the time. For years, American college students had played stickball informally, and a loose form of football—a soccerlike game descended from a game played in medieval times in English villages. In the late 1850s the different college classes started playing baseball against one another at Rutgers; and in 1869 the students of Rutgers and the students of Princeton met, worked out a compromise set of rules between the local rules of their informal football games, and inaugurated American intercollegiate football. They also began intercollegiate baseball and rowing, though Rutgers was too poor to keep crew going until much later, and started intercollegiate track later in the century. College loyalty was expressed by other sorts of intercollegiate aggressiveness as well, most notably by the "Cannon War" with Princeton in 1875. Rutgers students sneaked down to Princeton one night and stole a cannon said to have been taken from New Brunswick on an earlier occasion. Princeton students counter-attacked, and the whole town of New Brunswick protected the Rutgers students; according to one story, a local judge hid the stolen cannon. Eventually the presidents of Rutgers and Princeton had to appoint a faculty committee to settle the war.

Late-nineteenth-century intercollegiate football was a hairy business. It was played without protective gear and involved massive collisions between increasingly well-coached formations. Some of the teams Rutgers played regularly—Princeton in particular—soon became major football powers, and Rutgers regularly served itself up to them for slaughter. In one particularly tough encounter in 1892, Princeton decided to eliminate the largest Rutgers player, Frank Grant, which according to an alumnus's memory a Princeton player "very effectively accomplished by running forward and throwing himself face down and crosswise to the approaching wedge. Grant stepped directly between [his] legs where his foot was held fast and the momentum and weight of the wedge did the rest. The result was a clean square fracture of both bones of the leg a few inches above the ankle." As he was carried away, Grant was rumored to have said, "I'd die for dear old Rutgers." (In one version of the legend, a Princeton player responded, "Die, then!") The saying—"I'd die for dear old Rutgers"—attained some general fame in later years as the slogan for valiant and sometimes futile college spirit. The Broadway show *High Button Shoes* satirized it with the song "Nobody Ever Died for Dear Old Rutgers." Rutgers' central role in early intercollegiate football probably has as much to do with its subsequent Ivy League–like reputation outside the state of New Jersey as does its colonial founding.

Late-nineteenth-century Rutgers students' energies went mostly into collegiate matters, but occasionally the students addressed themselves to wider issues. Politically they tended to be Republicans, like their elders. In 1881, when President Garfield suffered a lingering death as a result of an assassin's bullet in nearby Elberon, New Jersey, the whole town of New Brunswick went into mourning—with the exception of the editor of the local Democratic newspaper. In outrage, a large mob of Rutgers students surrounded his house one night and subjected him to abuse.

As a distinctive collegiate outlook developed among Rutgers students, the formal value of academic achievement became increasingly unimportant. Early-nineteenth-century students had competed eagerly for academic honors, and generally an "honors man" was very much admired by his peers—unless he was suspected of getting honors unfairly by being a "bootlicker." Late-nineteenth-century students gave their admiration to the football player or even more to the all-around good fellow—the "brick" in the college slang of the 1870s. A member of the Class of 1868, looking back from the vantage point of 1916, remembered that "we held the college life in high esteem, and properly condemned merely class-room success and high marks and any currying of favor with professors to that end."

By 1890, according to his student diary, the average, fun-loving student Horace Hawes spent a characteristic two-week period studying or "reading" five times; "fooling around," "bumming around," or "scrapping" thirteen times; visiting young ladies three times; attending church four times; going to bars or the theater five times; playing cards twice; traveling out of town twice; and singing, shooting, and attending the Junior Ball once. Hawes's organized extracurricular activities were equally vigorous; he also attended fraternity, college class, and literary society meetings, worked on the *Targum*, and traveled with the baseball team as its scorekeeper. According to the yearbooks, the two hundred or so undergraduates at the college in the 1890s supported at least as many extracurricular organizations as do the almost eight thousand students at Rutgers college in the 1980s. Of course, late-nineteenth-century Rutgers students did not work nearly as hard academically. Numerical grading was instituted in the 1860s, but it was not very stiff. The lowest four-year average of the class of 1866 was 77.5 and the median was 90.5. "The College was then seeking students, instead of students seeking college," an 1885 alumnus remembered eighty years later, adding that every single student he referred to Rutgers in later years "President Scott and President Demarest graciously granted scholarships, I do not know why or how."

It was probably tougher to be a college authority in the late nineteenth century than in the earlier years of the century. In an era when most of the faculty still lived around the college, unpopular professors were sometimes visited at night by gangs of students with washtubs and other noisemakers and were subjected to a "Callithumpian serenade." Students demonstrated their class loyalty by cutting ("sloping") particular classes en masse. In 1867 the entire student body, led by the future Rutgers trustee T. G. Bergen, rioted over the faculty's refusal to install a gate in the campus fence opposite the literary society rooms in Van Nest Hall. In the late 1870s the juniors terrified one professor with the "gun riot," emptying the armory of the rifles they used in military drill and surrounding him threateningly in a classroom. Merrill Gates, a new, young president, took over in 1882 and attempted to crack down, pledging not to tolerate the old "schoolboy ethics" (which in fact had only developed at Rutgers in the 1860s). Gates appealed to the students' "honor," suppressed the cane rush, threatened to call in the police against student disorders, and on one occasion forbade student participation in a minstrel show on the grounds that it was beneath their dignity as "gentlemen." Gates's patriarchal approach failed, however, alienating most of the students and many of the alumni, and he departed unlamented in 1892; he is virtually the only person from nineteenth-century Rutgers who does not have a building named after him in the modern university.

The president and the faculty pursued subtler means thereafter. In the 1890s a joint faculty-student disciplinary committee was formed, but due to student politics and faculty manipulation, it did not work. In 1901 the students joined the faculty in calling for the appointment of a "cool, clear-headed, tactful Dean," and a new era began. Student autonomy was further hedged and limited by other institutional changes in the next twenty years. Since 1890 students had for the first time lived under a college-controlled roof, in the new dorm—Winant's Hall—which housed eighty undergraduates. After 1910 the university began to exert control over the other places many of them lived, over the fraternities (which had now increased to thirteen). After 1900 public-relations and alumni-relations officers joined the staff of the college; no longer did undergraduates have a monopoly on defining the nature of college life in the pages of the *Targum* and the *Scarlet Letter*. Other publications appeared: the YMCA began producing a handbook for incoming students about 1900, and the *Rutgers Alumni Quarterly* inaugurated alumni publications in 1914. And after 1910 the college began to take over intercollegiate sports, hiring professional coaches and eventually installing an athletics department as part of the faculty. As it did at other colleges, the late nineteenth century lived on in Rutgers alumni's memory as the golden age of undergraduate collegiate life, as a time of fun and real freedom. At just the time when students' lives were becoming more effectively managed by adult authorities, college had come to stand in the popular imagination as a place of adolescent fun, increasing the appeal of college to youths in the subsequent periods of mass college education.

The student profile also began to change at Rutgers around 1900. Until the end of the century, the college had continued to draw its students from old Protestant stock in the original Dutch areas of New York and New Jersey, educating declining but still significant proportions of preclerical students (24 percent of the undergraduates went into the clergy in 1890–1891, as compared to a pre–Civil War average of 36 percent), and more who went into such new professions as engineering, or into business. In the early twentieth century, as Rutgers grew and became more identified with the state of New Jersey, the recruitment area changed to what it is at present—mostly North Jersey. More incoming students were Jewish and Catholic, reflecting the waves of eastern and southern European immigration into the Northeast in the late nineteenth century. And more students were from lower socioeconomic classes. According to Richard P. McCormick, 80 percent of the incoming students in 1886 were from private schools; by 1916, 82 percent were from public high schools.

Other things also began to change quickly at Rutgers after the turn of the century. Rutgers faculty, like college faculty elsewhere, had been redefining themselves as a "profession" since the 1880s; the clergyman-professors had been replaced by professional academics, most of them with advanced degrees in their subjects, as likely to identify with the new "departments" as with the college as a whole. More slowly than comparable schools, Rutgers dropped the old mandatory classical curriculum; limited electives were instituted in 1888, and more extensive ones in 1907. The era of extensive faculty research did not come for many more years, though from the 1890s the Agricultural Experiment Station attracted some outstanding scholars. Also in the 1890s much more federal money became available to American colleges (three-fifths of the Rutgers budget in the mid-1890s was federal money, according to McCormick), and in 1904 Rutgers won an important legal case legitimizing state-funded scholarships at the college. A wealthy New Brunswick citizen,

▼
LITHOGRAPH OF CAMPUS, 1879
By 1879, the Old Queen's campus looked almost
as it does today; Winants Hall was added later,
and the President's house was eventually replaced by a parking lot. Kirkpatrick Chapel (1873)
is a fine example of Gothic Revival, and Geological Hall (1871)—balancing it on the other side
of Old Queen's—also has Gothic elements.
Along with Van Nest and the especially fine little
Schanck observatory (1866), the Old Queen's
assemblage was architecturally distinguished by
nineteenth-century standards, and remains the
architectural high point of the university. This
lithograph is composed like a photograph, with
its street-filled foreground—it is rare for a
nineteenth-century lithograph such as this not to
be drawn from a "bird's eye view." Compared to
the 1847 lithograph in Chapter 1 (p. 12), in this
picture the vegetation has grown considerably.

James Neilson '66, chose the occasion of President Demarest's inauguration in 1906
to donate the land for what until recently was called the Neilson Campus, the block
bounded by Hamilton Streets, Seminary Place, College Avenue, and George Street,
and a new phase of building began: Ballantine Gym in 1890, Voorhees Library in
1902, the Engineering and Chemistry buildings (now Murray and Milledoler) in
1909 and 1910, the Administration Building (now Martin Hall) at the Agricultural
Experiment Station in 1914, and the second dorm, Ford Hall, in 1915. As at other
colleges at this time, the controlling agency for this new complexity, the administration, expanded rapidly. Irving Upson had been the first non-faculty staff member
aside from the janitor, filling a variety of posts from librarian to secretary to the
faculty for twenty-five years beginning in the 1880s. By 1916 there was an administrative staff of fifteen reporting to the president of Rutgers.

In 1916, as World War I approached, the college celebrated its 150th anniversary with several days of ceremony. President Demarest was a member of an old
Dutch family, the fourth generation in his family connected with Rutgers, and the
author of the first Rutgers history. The pageantry emphasized Rutgers tradition with
music and tableaux fancifully reenacting historical moments relevant to the college,
and guests were invited from other colonially founded colleges. In his extended remarks on Rutgers, Demarest referred only occasionally and vaguely to the "future
progress" of the institution. Rutgers was being pulled reluctantly into the state-
college identity implicit in its land-grant status; for at least thirty more years, it
would remain an unusually mixed institution.

▼
GEORGE H. COOK
A modern image of an inspired George H. Cook creating Rutgers as a land-grant institution in 1864.
Cook was the first full-time, non-clerically trained faculty member at Rutgers. When he was hired in
1853, he was privately appalled at the lethargy of the existing faculty members. All of them except
Cook were purged when the trustees shook up the institution in the mid-1850s. Cook made the critical
difference in Rutgers' fight with Princeton for land-grant designation; due to his experience as assistant
state geologist, he knew the state better than anyone at Princeton, and he and the professor of mathematics, David Murray, did the necessary lobbying of the legislature. Later Cook established the Agricultural Experiment Station on the College Farm. He was by far the most important single figure at
nineteenth-century Rutgers.

WINANTS HALL

After years of lobbying against the anti-dormitory prejudices of nineteenth-century college authorities (finance was also a problem), the students finally got their first real dorm in 1890, Winants Hall. Architecturally, it is an eclectic neoclassical building. For twenty-five years, the students were very sentimental about the building, the first one that had really belonged to them:

At the end of the campus, stately and tall,
Rises the structure of fair Winants Hall
                    (*Scarlet Letter*, 1894)

Many of the student group photos around the turn of the century were taken on the steps of Winants, which currently houses the economics department. Under its recent refurbishing can be seen such original homey details as a marble hallway and fireplaces.

▲
An architect's rendering, probably drawn before the building was complete.

▶
A photograph, about 1910, of Winants, Van Nest with its third story, and Geological Hall.

▼
New Brunswick, 1884
A section from a panorama of New Brunswick,
taken in 1884 from the top of the 140-foot-spire
of the First Reformed Church on Neilson Street by
George Parsell, a professional photographer and
architect. This picture looks toward Rutgers,
which is not visible in the trees in the center back.
"E" and "J" mark Hertzog Hall and Suydam Hall
at the Seminary. The Johnson & Johnson factories
are visible in the upper right.

"Riverstead," 1880s

The house at 542 George Street, still standing on the corner of Seminary Place, was designed and built by George Cook in the late 1860s and soon sold to the Theological Seminary. The resident when this photo was taken is not known; President Demarest lived in the house after his retirement in 1924, and died there in 1956. Van Nest Hall, in the background, is without its third story, none of the Neilson Campus is built, and electricity has not yet replaced gas lighting. This is an interestingly posed photo, with the man of the house returning home through the gate, the women of the household awaiting him, and a seemingly disconsolate child in the yard.

Kirkpatrick Library

The Rutgers library two buildings ago. Before Voorhees was built in 1902 (the predecessor to the current Alexander Library), Kirkpatrick Chapel had a gallery about eighteen feet up in the current sanctuary which housed books. This is probably a late-nineteenth-century photo.

NEW JERSEY HALL

New Jersey Hall was finished in 1889 in high Victorian style. Its architect was the aerial photographer, George Parsell. The first of the buildings in the later expansion northwest out of the Old Queen's Campus, it was originally intended for agricultural education and belonged to the state rather than to the college.

▲
A late-nineteenth-century photo. The electrical pole in the foreground indicates a later date than the photo of "Riverstead" (p. 39).

▶
New Jersey Hall burned in 1903 but was quickly restored.

▶
Bird's-eye-view Lithograph of
New Brunswick, 1910
A detail of a 1910 bird's-eye-view lithograph of
New Brunswick shows the industrial development of the town since the 1845 lithograph was
drawn (pp. 8–9). It also shows Rutgers' early-
twentieth-century growth: the new Neilson
Campus (in the block below the words "College Avenue"), with Ballantine Hall, Voorhees
Hall, and the buildings now called Murray
and Milledoler; and the Rutgers Athletic Field
(Neilson Field). The second dorm, Ford Hall, is
not yet built, and Bishop House still stands in its
glade of trees. At this time, civic boosters took
pride in the industrial smokiness of their factories, as the Johnson & Johnson stacks right next
to the college indicate. In photographs of the
city taken every decade or so after Parsells's
1884 panorama, one can see ever-increasing air
pollution.

▼
Trolley, 1906
From the 1890s until the 1920s, trolleys ran
through the streets near the college. This one
has stopped at the intersection of Hamilton and
Easton in 1906, still in prepavement days.

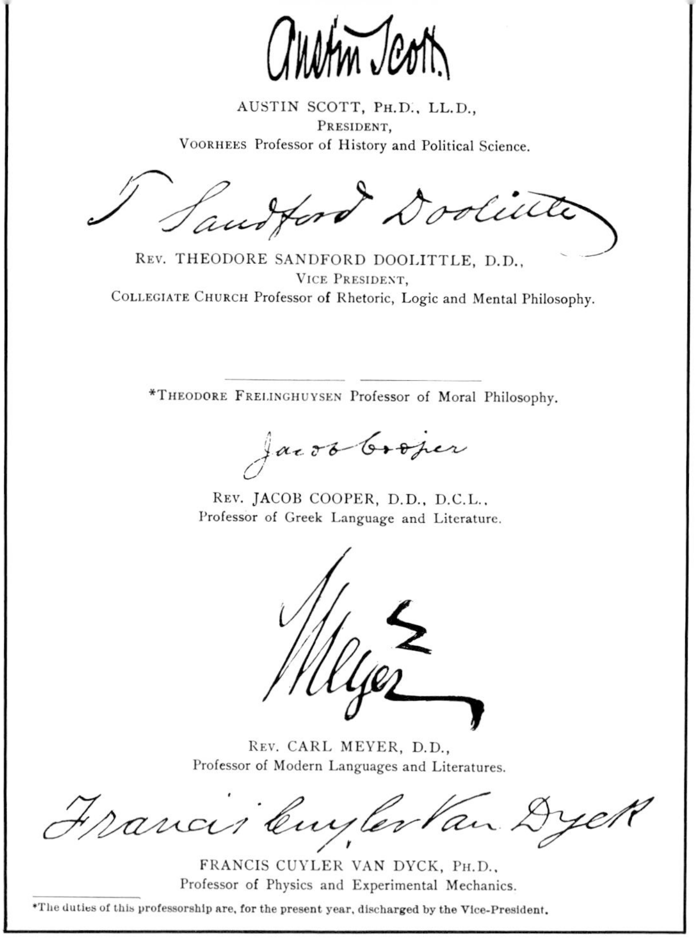

Austin Scott

AUSTIN SCOTT, PH.D., LL.D.,
PRESIDENT,
VOORHEES Professor of History and Political Science.

T Sandford Doolittle

REV. THEODORE SANDFORD DOOLITTLE, D.D.,
VICE PRESIDENT,
COLLEGIATE CHURCH Professor of Rhetoric, Logic and Mental Philosophy.

*THEODORE FRELINGHUYSEN Professor of Moral Philosophy.

Jacob Cooper

REV. JACOB COOPER, D.D., D.C.L.,
Professor of Greek Language and Literature.

Meyer

REV. CARL MEYER, D.D.,
Professor of Modern Languages and Literatures.

Francis Cuyler Van Dyck

FRANCIS CUYLER VAN DYCK, PH.D.,
Professor of Physics and Experimental Mechanics.

*The duties of this professorship are, for the present year, discharged by the Vice-President.

▶
FACULTY SIGNATURES, 1891
This page of faculty signatures appeared in the
1891 yearbook.

STUDENT'S PROGRESS, 1887
Climbing the perilous stairs to academic
success—a student's view. Given the relative
ease of getting through Rutgers at the time, this
is somewhat melodramatic. The names of the
stairs, bottom to top, represent the freshman-to-
senior mandatory curriculum ("Freeman," near
the bottom, was a text often burned in sophomore cremations). "Conditions" were limitations on a particular promotion; a student might
be promoted to the junior year on the condition
that he hire a tutor during vacation to make up
some deficiency. The faculty plays the music
while a few victorious students at the top climb
the Phi Beta Kappa flagpole.

STUDENTS AND FACULTY, 1900
Perhaps half the students (arranged by class)
and faculty posed for this group photo in the
portico of Winants Hall around 1900. President
Austin Scott is in the front center, a paper in his
left hand.

▶
Academic Groups

The sciences generated more excitement among students in the 1880s and 1890s than did the humanities, and the few surviving photos that show students in any sort of academic context are science groups. This photo from the early 1890s shows a student lab group with professors. The students are wonderfully diverse in dress and pose. A few of them are in the Civil War military uniforms worn by the cadets. Science lab was a great place to pick up things with interesting extracurricular uses: skulls, handy chemicals, mild explosives. The photo is unusual in showing the faculty behind the students. Fifth from the left at the top (short, with porkpie hat) is Professor Julius Nelson, a zoologist who initiated oyster research at Rutgers and in the state; right of him (in a bowler hat) is Professor John B. Smith, an entomologist who pioneered New Jersey mosquito research.

THIRD LETTER.

RUTGERS COLLEGE,

New Brunswick, N. J.,————————*188* .

Dear ———————— *;*

Your ———— *has* ———— *absences (one tardiness, except from Preaching, counts as one-half an absence) recorded against him, of which* ———— *are unexcused, as follows :*

	Absences.	Tardinesses.
Bible-class on Sunday,	–	–
Preaching " "	–	–
Morning Prayers,	–	–
Recitation,	–	–
Total,	–	–

Very Respectfully,

Secretary of the Faculty.

EXTRACT FROM THE STANDING RULES.

1. Absences or tardinesses for which excuse is not rendered by the student within one week, are entered as unexcused.

2. An absence from Chapel preaching on Sunday counts as two absences from recitation ; an absence from Bible-class as one absence from recitation.

3. All students are required to attend the religious services, including Bible-class, at Chapel on Sunday, except those whose parents or guardians wish them to attend worship with some other denomination than the Reformed ; and in all such cases the wish must be expressed to the President in writing, at the beginning of each term.

4. When a student has received 6 marks of unexcused absence and misconduct, or of either, the Secretary of the Faculty shall notify the parent of such student of the fact. When he has received 6 more marks of like character, a second notice shall be sent to the parent. When he has received 18 marks, a third notice shall be sent, and the student admonished by the President. When 24 are recorded against him, he shall be dismissed or suspended from the College.

▶
Deficiency Form

After the 1860s the college began to do bureaucratically those things which hitherto it had done personally. This form from the 1880s standardizes absences from class ("Recitation"), from daily chapel ("Morning prayers"), and from Sunday services ("Bible-class," "Preaching"). With a total of eighteen absences, a student was personally "admonished" by the president; with twenty-four, he was thrown out, temporarily at least.

▶
AGRICULTURAL CLASS
Ed Lipman '33, currently a trustee of Rutgers, says, "I can tell you exactly when this picture was taken—I never saw my father when he had so much hair!" The photo shows a student group about 1910, with Jacob Lipman at the center rear, with mustache (the child is not one of Lipman's). Lipman was then an instructor; in 1914, he became the vigorous founding dean of the College of Agriculture.

林玄助 Hiase

杉南弘蔵 Soogiwooree

津田鹽太郎 Tseeda

児玉菫二郎 Kodama

日本諸生ヲニウブランスウィキ滞在ノ間モル井氏ニ呈ス

The Japanese Students in New Brunswick present this to Prof & Mrs Murray.

橋口宗伐 Hashiguti

花岡武郎 Maruoka

島津久之進 Prince Shimads

◄
JAPANESE STUDENTS
Rutgers is historically important as the first American college in which Japanese students enrolled during the Japanese modernizing period that followed the Meiji restoration in the late 1860s. A few Reformed Church missionaries to Japan had provided the initial contacts. In this photo taken in 1870 for Professor and Mrs. David Murray, who later went to Japan as educators, an early group of Japanese students have westernized their apparel remarkably faithfully. The proud youth with the cane, sitting second from the right, is Prince Matanoshiu Skimatsu, "son of the Lord of the former Sadohara clan," who did not actually attend Rutgers. Dozens of Japanese alumni went on to important positions in the Japanese government. William Griffis '69, like Murray, went to Japan as an educator and became an important early Western observer.

▲
GRAVES OF JAPANESE STUDENTS
Early Japanese students at Rutgers were not immunologically prepared for New Jersey. This is a pretty nook of the Willow Brook cemetery in downtown New Brunswick, as restored for a Japanese delegation in the 1970s. Some of the young men buried here were Rutgers students in the 1870s and 1880s. Others were Japanese who had died in New York City. One stone marks the grave of a child of a Rutgers student.

THE BRAHMINS
AND THEIR LITERATURE.

Rev. Henry Martyn Scudder, D. D.,

Will deliver the Annual Address before the

Philoclean and Peithessophian

LITERARY SOCIETIES,
On Tuesday, June 22,
AT 3 P. M.,
In Kirkpatrick Chapel.

This lecture affords an opportunity for exhibiting the characteristics of the ingenious and versatile Brahmin race, and for giving specimens of their fondness for alliteration in making verses. " They are as mirth provoking as they are curious." All are cordially invited to attend and bring " their sisters and their cousins and their aunts " and other friends with them. It is desired to give the doctor a welcome worthy of his brilliant reputation as an orator, and of the rich entertainment which his rare treatment of an attractive theme will offer.

COME EARLY SO AS TO SECURE SEATS.

◄
ANOTHER RUTGERS MISSIONARY CONNECTION
The Scudder family worked in Ceylon and India in the nineteenth and twentieth centuries and sent fifteen young men to Rutgers before 1916. They founded what is one of the finest hospitals in south India, in Vellore, and one of them made a key discovery in the ethnography of kinship for the anthropological pioneer Lewis Henry Morgan. Henry Martyn Scudder had been given an honorary D.D. degree by Rutgers in 1859. This lecture was given in the 1880s.

▶
JAMES DICKSON CARR
So far as is known, James Dickson Carr '92, was the first black graduate of Rutgers. He was the son of a Presbyterian clergyman from Elizabeth, New Jersey, and he later went to Columbia Law School and became an assistant district attorney in New York City. On an alumni form after graduation he listed his avocation as "hard work."
It could not have been easy to be a black undergraduate at Rutgers in the late nineteenth century. An alumnus, remembering Carr's college days in Carr's obituary in 1920, claimed that he was held in "respect" by the other students, but added "if any one was inclined to pass him by because of his color, Carr at least would not notice it . . . his social life in college was not wide, although every one who called on him . . . always received a hearty welcome." Carr's only surviving major communication with Rutgers in his alumni file is a strong protest to President Demarest about Rutgers' keeping Paul Robeson out of a football game with Washington and Lee in 1916, because the Washington and Lee team objected to playing against a black man. If the president made any response, it has not survived.

After about 1860 the college class became an important social group, and well into the twentieth century students of a class had their pictures taken together.

▼

The Class of 1875 was photographed by the side of the newly completed Kirkpatrick Chapel, with President Campbell seated in the center. Late-nineteenth- and early-twentieth-century classes placed stones recording their class years in the side of Kirkpatrick, and planted ivy beneath them. For young men in the 1870s, stylish top hats and derbies, elegant mustaches, and canes marked their adult status. Students who could not grow mustaches were mocked, and freshmen who wore hats or carried canes were hazed or threatened with the "cane rush" or "hat rush."

▶

The Class of 1891, in a cheeky pose in front of a bar and billiards hall, possibly on Burnet Street downtown. The unorthodox setting was probably facilitated by the photographer's being a member of the class (note the photographic trip wire that the man in the front right is holding). The new diversity of hats and clothing indicates the developing elaboration and self-consciousness of collegiate groups; unlike students in the 1875 class photo, these young men wear youthful college dress rather than clothing characteristic of any fashionable adults. The class hats with class numerals on them are starting to come into fashion, but these look like homemade affairs.

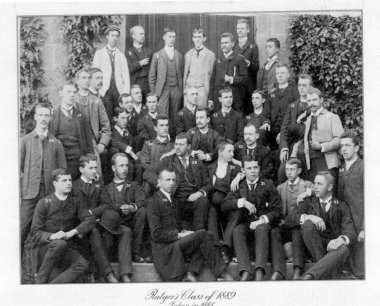

Rutgers Class of 1889
Taken in 1885

1. JOHN O. POLAK ×   2. BYRON CUMMINGS   3. FRANK H. SKINNER   4. GEORGE V. W. DURYEE ×   5. GEORGE B. THOMPSON ×   6. CHARLES J. SCUDDER
7. KUMAKICHIRO OISHI   8. WILLIAM L. DAYTON ×   9. JOSEPH S. STILLWELL ×   10. ISAAC M. HOLLY ×   11. HAROLD D. FORCE   12. RICHARD T. GREENE
13. B. HASBROUCK   14. JOHN T. E. DE WITT   15. MAURICE J. THOMPSON ×   16. GEORGE J. STEINMETZ   17. WILLIAM C. SEBRING   18. WILLIAM W. HALLOCK
19. JOHN P. STREET   20. EDWARD HOWELL   21. CHARLES MAAR   22. JAMES H. KEELING, JR.   23. HARVEY S. LOSEE ×   24. ARTHUR J. COLLIER ×
25. CLARENCE O. SCUDDER ×   26. ALBERT C. ARENDT ×   27. ALBERT B. HARRISON   28. SAM. C. SCHENCK   29. GEORGE MORRIS ×   30. GEORGE A. LIGGETT ×
31. WILLIAM S. MYERS ×   32. CHARLES B. BENSON ×   33. JAMES H. LE FEVRE ×   34. ELIAS W. THOMPSON

▲

The Class of 1889 as freshmen, most with their hats respectfully off their heads.

▼
Photographic printing advances around the turn of the century made it feasible for the Class of 1900 to adopt the modern yearbook format, with individual pictures and biographical information.

▶
CLASS ICONOGRAPHY, 1886
As college class solidarity developed in the late nineteenth century, student artists modified the old "ages of man" allegorical drawings to characterize the college classes in ways that endured down to the 1930s or 1940s, and that occasionally still turn up in alumni ceremonies. In these beautiful renditions from the 1886 yearbook, the freshman is a precocious infant, the sophomore an overreaching ne'er-do-well, the junior a young rake, and the senior a mature man of the world. For fifty years, the "class histories" reinforced the same images, bragging about the pranks and foolishness of the first two years and claiming increasing seriousness thereafter.

Class of 1900.

"A COCK OFT CROWS WITHOUT A VICTORY."

SENIOR PERSONALIA.

ARTHUR PERLEE BROKAW..............................Freehold, N. J.

Δ Υ

Track Team (1, 2, 3, 4) ; Captain (4) ; Gymnasium Team (2, 3, 4) ; Class Foot-Ball Team (3, 4) ; Junior Orator.

"A thing of beauty and a joy forever."

CLARENCE EDWARDS CASE............................Somerville, N. J.

Δ Υ, Φ B K

Freshman, Sophomore and Junior Orator; Speaker of Congress; Debating Team (4) ; Presenter of Mementoes, Class Day; First Classical Honor.

"He mouths a sentence as curs mouth a bone."

ROBERT ANDERSON COOKE.......................New Brunswick, N. J.

Δ K E, Θ N E, Cap and Skull.

Winner of Perlee Junior Orator Prize; Debating Team (4) ; Speaker of Congress.

"What makes life dreary is the lack of motive."

CHARLES TIEBOUT COWENHOVEN, JR............New Brunswick, N. J.

Δ Φ, Cap and Skull.

"Prouder than rustling in unpaid-for silk."

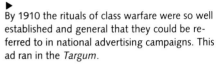

By 1910 the rituals of class warfare were so well established and general that they could be referred to in national advertising campaigns. This ad ran in the *Targum*.

CLASS WARFARE
Warfare between classes started in the 1860s and continued in various forms for one hundred years or more.

▲
The Class of 1885's celebration of its victories over '84, in various skirmishes in the halls of Old Queen's.

▶
In the early 1880s President Gates, caricatured here protecting the tiny freshman ("'87") from the sophomore ("'86"), suppressed the cane rush. To the students, this amounted to the death of "college life." The insert commemorates a hazing incident perpetrated by '86.

► A 1966 revival of the proc genre, self-consciously archaic, done when the freshman "dinks" had become voluntary and were within about three years of dying out entirely.

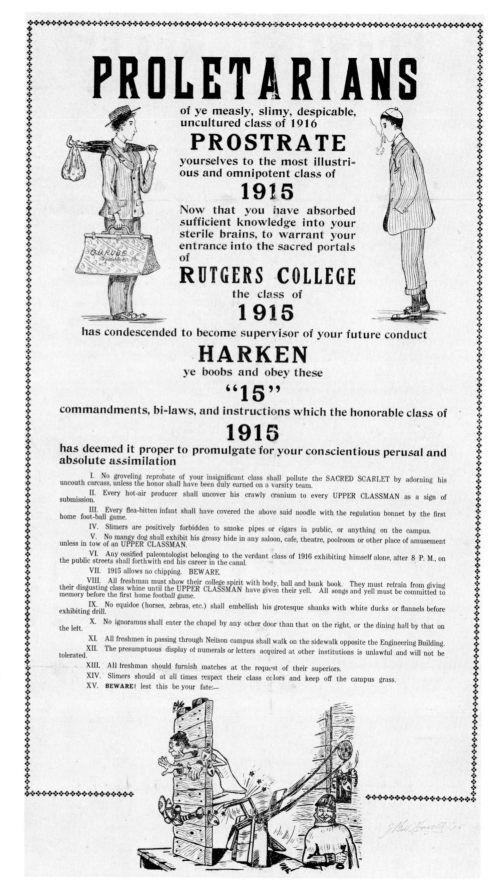

► In the 1890s sophomores started printing proclamations prohibiting the freshmen from enjoying certain privileges; sometimes the freshmen fought back with their own "procs," and "proc rushes" ensued. Initially, enforcement of the procs was up to the sophomores; later, the college took over the system and made the freshman prohibitions official (though actual enforcement was still generally a sophomore prerogative). The proclamations were printed regularly until about 1930. They are a vivid key to the times; as the things that stood for adulthood or fashionable adolescence changed, so did the prohibitions. In the 1890s high hats and canes were forbidden to freshmen. In this 1915 example white ducks and flannels were out. In 1931 knickers, golf stockings, and fancy sweaters were not to be worn.

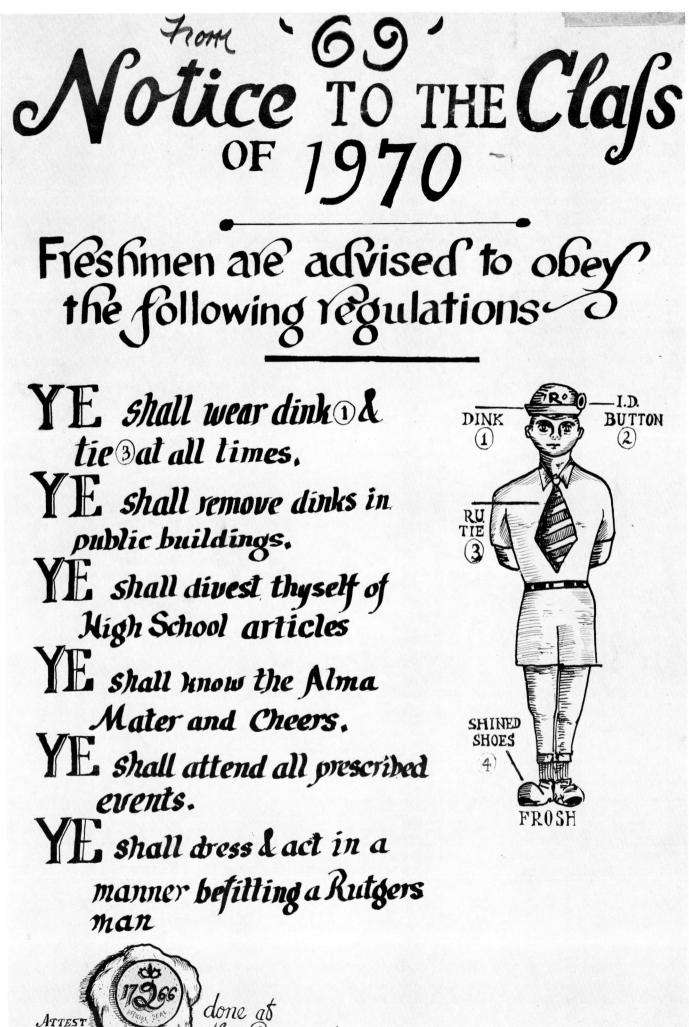

STUDENT LIFE AT NEW-BRUN-SWICK.

MY VISITORS.

FIRST in importance come the students who are of the same secret persuasion as myself. These call upon me at all hours of the day and night, and labor under the sad delusion that nothing in my *own* room is sacred to myself, but is placed there for the benefit of them all. They make it a point to write all their letters here, and always inquire coolly for postage-stamps. They throw themselves upon the bed with perfect reckless-ness, boots and all, and I have known four of them to be on it at one time struggling for the possession of a pillow. When smoking, they are oblivious to the use of a spittoon, although I be-lieve that one fellow, in an attempt to get off a borrowed joke, *did* remark one afternoon "that if I did not take that thing away he would spit in it." But after all, I am always glad to see them. Better, far better, to have a friend that uses you for his convenience than not to have a friend at all.

Another class of visitors are those fellows who just step in to borrow your notes. When a per-son does this, and says he has been absent from recitations, and so was unable to obtain the lec-ture, I willingly excuse him, and place every scrap of information I am possessed of in his hands. But when he says he "did not take notes this time," I do not refuse him mine, but I set him down for a beat, defunct at that. Why should he not take notes as well as anybody else? The plan of living off your neighbors is a very antiquated one, but its disciples are very numer-ous in this world of ours. There are plenty of men both *in* college and *out* who will shirk every particle of labor, except that which they are *obliged* to perform.

Another visitor who frequently drops in upon me is the student from another college. *He* comes merely to give you a chance to show your hospi-tality. Never be alarmed, my young collegian, of overdoing the matter. I have found that the stranger student is always willing to take all you give him, and when he departs, any little memen-to of his visit that you may hand him will be thankfully received. There is only one way to repay their kind attentions, and that is always to return the visit. This intimacy between stu-dents of different colleges should certainly be en-couraged, and I think that the trustees of "Rut-gers" should set aside a portion of their recent donations to be used as a fund for paying the ex-penses of students from other colleges who might choose to visit any of their friends in this glorious institution. But to resume. Once and awhile I re-ceive a visit from "ye bore." "Ye bore," is a gent who smokes, but never carries cigars; talks, but has no ideas of his own, and thinks that Pegasus was not a horse but a mud-turtle. Unlike the bore of Sydney Smith's celebrated definition, he seldom talks about himself, but abounds in old jokes with no point; is fond of resurrecting old discussions and ideas, and of the numerous paths through life is acquainted with but one. He "never could see any fun in boating," and thinks "the study of mathematics is horrible." Greek, however, he is fond of. He may be known at the dining-table by his continually asking for more gravy, and at college he always uses a half-inch lead pencil. Those are strange and varied char-acteristics, but they are undoubtedly true ones. Whenever you see a student that will answer to this description, shun him. Never invite him to your room, for if you do he will most certainly come and your patience will be severely tried be-fore you can get rid of him. Other kinds of vis-itors often drop in upon me, but a brief notice of them is all that I have time to give. First comes the student who considers "making calls" a duty imposed upon all true collegians. I like that student. He generally calls in the evening, chats pleasantly for half an hour, and then takes his departure, inviting me to return his visit at my earliest convenience, and moreover, he does not call again until I have done so. Next comes the fellow who wants to know "where Atherton commences." This, to the uninitiated may seem a strange question, but permit me to explain that in student phraseology the name of the professor and the lesson recited in his room are synony-mous terms. Strange and outer visitors often call upon me without premonition. I once had a visit from a parrot, who had escaped from a cage which hung against an adjacent house. I tried to domesticate the bird in an old cigar box, but he made such a horrible noise during the night that I was forced to release him. Cats nightly visit an old box which lies beneath my window, and there express their views in a catachrestic man-ner. I have found, however, that throwing hot ashes from my window upon their heads effectu-ally destroys the harmony of the meeting.

Let me now leave this part of my subject and speak of the sights that can be seen from my win-dow. I have noticed that all dwellers in cities are possessed of the strange fallacy that when they once get in their own seven-by-nine back yard, no human eye can behold their 'actions. Again and again has it been proved that they are deceived, but they never abandon the idea. This is particularly the case with the inhabitants of the good city of New-Brunswick. My room be-ing a rear one, I have an excellent view of the yards belonging to at least a score of houses. I am compelled to state that the scenery is not ro-mantic. Neither is it awe inspiring. But the various events which I have beheld take place in these said back-yards have amply rewarded me for the lack of beauty in the surrounding scenery. To thoroughly know human nature you must be-hold how persons act in their back-yards. This is a bit of homely but true advice. To occupy a back room in a house in the city is almost the same as possessing the power of Asmodeus. Let me describe some of the milder scenes that I have witnessed. There is an ice cream saloon directly opposite my window, and from many observations I have obtained an excellent idea of how our modern confectionery is made. But that is some-thing I do not intend to enlarge upon. The old proverb about "ignorance" and "bliss" will al-ways be applicable to ice cream and its consu-mers. Next to the ice cream saloon resides a family who always work in their garden on Sun-day. I have often watched them Sunday after-noons putting in their early peas. They have one lone cherry tree in their yard, and when the dozen cherries, which it annually bears, have become ripe, the family celebrate the occasion by having

THE TARGUM.

Rutgers College.

Vol. VI.—No. 2.] NEW-BRUNSWICK, N. J., FEBRUARY, 1874. [TERMS—$1.50 Per Year.

The Student's Toast.

O, here's a toast, ye College mates,
　You'll e'er respond to hearty,
'Round festive board, where glasses ring,
　Or at the social party :
　　'Tis the standing toast
　　That pleases the most—
　　Who dares say its imprudent ?—
　　To the jolly girl,
　　The frolicsome girl,
　　The girl that loves the student.

She may be blonde, perhaps brunette,
　Or even both combined ;
Among her charms the greatest is,
　Her gayety unconfined.
　　Then join in the toast
　　That pleases the most, &c.

The fragrance of the beauteous rose,
　The dew-drop's radiant rainbow,
The love divine of the student's girl,—
　Do these exist in vain ? No !
　　O, give us the toast
　　That pleases the most, &c.

We seek the sunshine of her smiles,
　When brain and eyes are weary :
Our homesick hearts she gladdens soon—
　Joys banish feelings dreary.
　　Then ring out the toast
　　That pleases the most, &c.

There's some do taunt, with jeering laugh,
　That she's a *rara avis ;*
It's rareness to the gold gives worth,
　And to our own dear mavis.
　　Hurrah for the toast
　　That pleases the most, &c.

We love the home we've left behind,
　Our hearts still there do linger ;
With joy we'd drink a toast to it,
　Of happiness harbinger.
　　But give us the toast
　　That pleases the most, &c.

Our Alma Mater, too, does hold
　A place in our affection—
To Rutgers gratitude shall swell,
　Whate'er be our connection.
　　Yet Rutgers, the toast
　　That pleases the most, &c.

The class tie unifies us all,
　We stand together ever ;
With real zest we drink the toast,
　"The class may't never sever."
　　But yet there's a toast
　　That pleases the most, &c.

Angelic woman, too, we'd toast ;
　Her praise has rung for ages ;
Self-sacrifice has always filled
　Her noble soul courageous.

Still better the toast
That pleases the most, &c.

The jovial song, the happy hit,
　Are relished each acutely ;
We toast the singer and the man
　Who flings sarcasm astutely.
　　We love more the toast
　　That pleases the most, &c.

Old age shall come—the past grow faint ;
　A light shall shine translucent,
In mem'ry's halls—thrice blessed light :
　The girl that loved the student.
　　'Tis memory's toast
　　Which pleases the most, &c.
　　　　　　　　GENNARO.

Some College Phrases.

To one unaccustomed to the usage or rehearsal of the *isms* of College, their frequent occurrence in the student's language must appear to him as a particular phraseology of a peculiar science. It is, indeed, a science, and one in which these technical terms figure with great significance. Science, *a la* Webster, is "truth ascertained," and when one truth becomes known, it is made the recipient of a specific name, to distinguish it clearly from other truths. The science in question, is the discovery of certain characteristics of persons, things and processes ; and when one characteristic has been established as identical with the characterized, it is given an appropriate name, and this name is indelibly jotted down as an exclusive and everlasting possession of the newly discovered phenomenon. Its votaries are continually astonishing the world by their achievements in discoveries, and the vocabulary of the applied names is swelling immensely. The lovers of this science are almost innumerable, and we can truthfully declare that it is studied more indefatigably during every College life than any other of the known sciences. To our knowledge, its technicalities have never been exhibited in print; and although we are not sure about other Colleges, we are justified in saying so of the field of Rutgers, they be-

ing handed down from generation to generation here, like the popular writings of the ancients, by word of mouth only. They ought to be collected from the various fields, properly classified, and published in book form, entitled " *An Exhaustive Treatise on College-Word Curiosities.*" It would make an exceedingly interesting volume, and its publication would undoubtedly be hailed with delight by all philologists, philomaths, and philanthropists. We can safely say that the book will not appear in this decade, but as the public ought to be somewhat cognizant of the merits of the coming tome, we will give, as a criterion of its value, a notion of its transcendent quality, in the appended compendium of current popular phrases at Rutgers.

Alumnus, a graduate; Bag, to steal; Bang-up, first-class—glorious ; Blat, Chin, Cackle, Buzz, to " sound" a man for society or other purposes, to tease by useless talk. Blood, of aristocratic origin, a monied man ; Bleed, to get money or favors from another generally by shrewdness; Bone, to solicit; Bookworm, a self-denying fellow who deprives himself of healthy exercise that he may die early and bury himself and his great erudition in the grave of condign oblivion; Boot-lick, Supe, to flatter and lie for the accomplishment of an end—one who worships Professors as gods, and who eats dust from their feet for one-third of a mark—a sneak-thief; Bounce, to boot, to expel; Brick, a free-hearted, careless, fun-loving and good-natured fellow—a fellow of the period ; Broke, out of money; Bum, a lively spree ; Bust, an impecunious bum ; Cake, Flat, Pill, a shallow-brained fellow, over fond of girls, an egotistical fool; Calico, a female; Chapel, morning religious service; Cheek, brazen audacity; Chum, a room-mate; Cod, Lalligag, used as a verb, of which the participle is the process, which means fooling, deceiving

ENTRANCE AND LEAVE-TAKING
More nineteenth-century images of the college.

▶
The freshman entering, 1887.

▲
The senior leaving, 1881. [The factory smoke
outside the gate is *not* allegorical; see the 1910
lithograph (pp. 42–43).]

CREMATION

In the "cremation," the sophomores marched in a midnight mock funeral procession, carrying their least-favorite book, which they burned and buried with appropriate oratory. The cremation had existed at Harvard in the 1850s. Rutgers students adopted it in the 1860s and discontinued it about 1900, when the more diverse curriculum meant that the whole class no longer had a common despised text.

◄
Cremation announcements from the 1880s. Sometimes a least-favorite professor was also burned in effigy.

▲
The sophomore class dressed as Indians (thought to be an appropriate representation of their wildness) for their cremation in 1892. They burned "Anna Lytics the witch," perhaps working off some misogyny in the process. "She had spoiled their unity and peace and caused disunion and trouble in the tribe . . . while she was burning they chanted her funeral hymn . . . and finished by giving the class yell" (from an 1892 *Targum*).

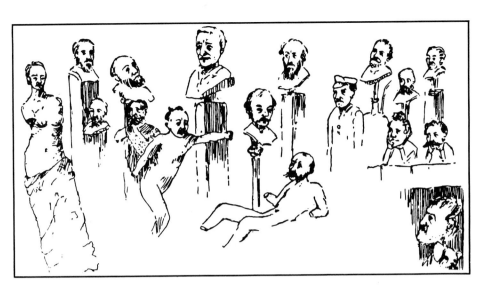

STUDENT ART
Advances in print lithography after the 1850s made elaborate illustrations feasible in student publications, and the 1870s and 1880s were the heyday of student drawing—which declined in the 1890s with the increased use of photography (facilitated in turn by the invention of the halftone plate). These examples show further how students developed the written burlesque genre of the early nineteenth century into more graphic assaults on the dignity of the faculty and the institution in the late nineteenth century.

▶
The faculty as classical nudes, 1882.

▲
Lab students disrupting the class of George Cook (left center, tearing hair), 1881.

▶
The real facts behind some standard excuses to the faculty, 1885.

▶▶
A "rake" by the freshmen, on the occasion of the generally rowdy Sophomore Exhibition in 1877. President ("Prex") Campbell sits at the head of the table. A "bob-tail flush" was a three-card flush in poker, good only for bluffing. This rake reached the attention of the trustees, who punished the class by canceling their Sophomore Exhibition the following year.

THE FACULTY BUST-ING.

Prex Holds a Bobtail Flush.

POETIC TRIBUTE TO THE POTENTATES OF RUTGERS.

"What makes the breaking of all oaths a holy duty? Food."—HUDIBRAS.

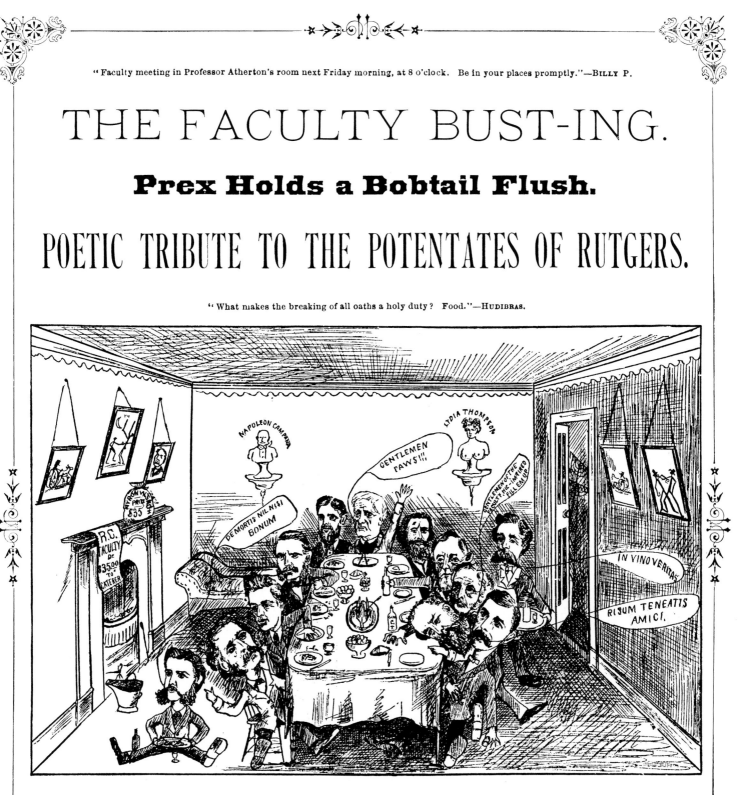

WASHINGTON'S BIRTHDAY, 1877.   THE FACULTY TAKES BOTH PRIZES.

"Bottles cracked in taverns—have much the sweeter kernels,
Than the sups allowed to us in the College Journals."

The entrance fee to this "free-for-all" shebang is ten per cent. of the purse, and no questions asked—by those who pay.

This is the only official commentary on the chief feature of the Exhibition, being published by order of the Trustees, the only body competent (?) to criticise the Faculty

A copy of this Poem bound in full Turkey morocco will be presented to the College Library, and the Librarian has promised on his honor as Professor, Politician, Lawyer, Tax Commissioner, Census Supervisor, Sunday School Superintendent, &c., &c., that he will put it on the shelf before the close of the century.

Even Alma Mater was not entirely safe from late-nineteenth-century student satire.

▶ "Before" (frontispiece of the 1888 yearbook).

Annuals, Colors and Yells of Prominent American Colleges.

College.	Annual.	Colors.	Yell.
Amherst College, Amherst, Mass.	Olio.	White and Purple.	Rah! Rah! Rah! Rah! Rah! Rah! Am-herst!
Brown University, Providence, R. I.	Liber Brunensis.	Brown.	Rah! Rah! Rah! Rah! Rah! Rah! Brown!
Columbia College, New York City.	Columbiad —The Miner.	Blue and White.	Hurrah! Hurrah! Hurrah! C-o-l-u-m-b-i-a!
College City of New York.	Microcosm.	Lavender.	Rah! Rah! Rah! C! C! N! Y!
Cornell University, Ithaca, N. Y.	Cornellian.	Red and White.	Cor-nell! I Yell! Yell! Yell! Cor-nell!
Dartmouth College, Hanover, N. H.	Ægis.	Green.	Wah-hoo-wah! Wah-hoo-wah! Da–d–d–dartmouth! Wah-hoo-wah! T-I-G-E-R!
Hamilton College, Clinton, N. Y.	Hamiltonian.	Pink.	Hurrah! Hurrah! Hurrah! Hamilton! Zip-rah-boom!
Harvard College, Cambridge, Mass.	Index.	Crimson.	Rah! Rah! Rah! Rah! Rah! Rah! Rah! Rah! Rah! Harvard!
Lafayette College, Easton, Pa.	Melange.	Maroon and White.	Rah! Rah! Rah! Tiger! Laf-a-yette!
Lehigh University, S. Bethlehem, Pa.	Epitome.	Blue and White.	Rah–le! Rah–high! Rah! Rah! Le-high!
Madison University, Hamilton, N. Y.	Salmagundi.	Magenta and Blue.	Rah! Rah! Rah! M-a-d-i-s-o-n!
University of Michigan, Ann Arbor, Mich.	Palladium.	Blue and Maize.	Rah! Rah! Rah! U. of M.!
Massachusetts Technical Institute, Boston, Mass.	Technique.	Cardinal and Gray.	Rah! Rah! Rah! Tech-nol-o-gy!

◄
And "after" (endpapers of the same yearbook).

Δ Φ   O   Z Ψ   O   Δ K E

College.	Annual.	Colors.	Yell.
University of Pennsylvania, Philadelphia, Pa.	Record.	Blue and Red.	Hurrah! Hurrah! Hurrah! Penn-syl-va-ni-a!
Princeton College, Princeton, N. J.	Bric-à-Brac.	Orange and Black.	Hurrah! Hurrah! Hurrah! Tiger! Siss! Boom! Ah!
Rensselaer Polytechnic Institute, Troy, N. Y.	Transit.	Cherry.	Rah! Rah! Rah! Rah! Rah! Rah! Rens-se-la-er!
University of Rochester, Rochester, N. Y.	Interpres.	Blue and Gray.	Hoi! Hoi! Hoi! Rah! Rah! Rah! Roch-es-ter!
Rutgers College, New Brunswick, N. J.	**Scarlet Letter.**	**Scarlet.**	**Rah! Rah! Rah! Bow-wow-wow! Rutgers!**
Stevens Technical Institute, Hoboken, N. J.	Eccentric–Bolt.	Cardinal and Gray.	Boom-rah! Boom-rah! Boom-rah! Stevens!
Trinity College, Hartford, Conn.	Ivy.	Green and White.	Trin-eye-tee! Trin-eye-tee! Trin-eye-tee!
University of Syracuse, Syracuse, N. Y.	Syracusan Onondagrean.	Pink and Blue.	Srah! Srah! Srah! Syr-a-cuse! Srah! Srah! Srah! Syr-a-cuse! Srah! Srah! Srah! Syr-a-cuse!
Tufts College, College Hill, Mass.	Brown and Blue.	Blue and Brown.	Hoop-la! Boom-yah! Rah! Rah! Tufts! Hoop-la! Boom-yah! Rah!
Union College, Schnectady, N. Y.	Garnet.	Garnet.	Rah! Rah! Rah! U-n-i-o-n! Hika! Hika! Hika!
Vassar College, Poughkeepsie, N. Y.	Harper's Bazaar.	Rose, Pink and Silvery Gray.	Rah! Rah! Rah! Yum! Yum! Yum! (Kiss! Kiss! Kiss!) Vassar!
Wesleyan College, Middletown, Conn.	Olla Podrida.	Lavender.	Rah! Rah! Rah! Wes-ley-an! Rah! Rah! Rah! Wes-ley-an! Rah! Rah! Rah! Wes-ley-an!
Williams College, Williamstown, Mass.	Gulielmensian.	Purple.	Ra! Ra! Ra! Williams! yams! yams! Williams!
Yale College, New Haven, Conn.	Banner Pot Pourri.	Blue.	Rah! Rah! Rah! Rah! Rah! Rah! Rah! Rah! Rah! Yale!

X Φ   X Ψ   Δ Υ

FRATERNITIES

Rutgers lifted its ban on the fraternities in 1864, and in the late nineteenth century the fraternities replaced the literary societies in students' affections. Their greater secrecy and their emphasis on social rather than intellectual skills accorded better with the values of late-nineteenth-century college life. After failing to suppress the fraternities between 1847 and 1864, college authorities made no real attempt to control them until after 1910.

▼
Whatever went on in the late-nineteenth-century fraternity initiation, it must have been frightening. From the 1880 yearbook.

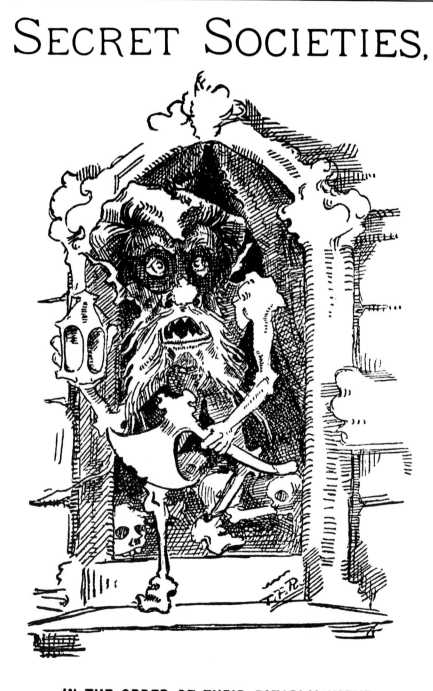

SECRET SOCIETIES,

IN THE ORDER OF THEIR ESTABLISHMENT.

▼
Zeta Psi around 1890. The reclining figure in the lower right is John Howard Raven, later a clergyman, trustee of Rutgers, and compiler of the 1916 catalog of all Rutgers alumni, 1766–1916.

▼
Chi Psi's lodge, one of the first two built, 1889.

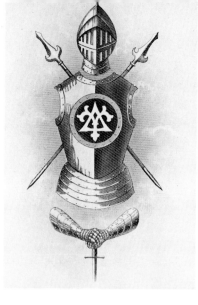

Between 1874 and 1882, Delta Upsilon changed from a high-minded ''Anti-Secret Society'' (its opponents liked to emphasize the acronym) to a fraternity like the others. The logos before and after. The 1882 logo anticipates the Rutgers Scarlet Knight.

A Zeta Psi house party in 1910, with an older woman chaperone and young ladies sitting discreetly separate from the men.

Theta Nu Epsilon's yearbook photo, 1908. The pledges were apparently in appropriate postures. The fraternity is now defunct at Rutgers.

FOOTBALL

Rutgers is famous for its role in the first intercollegiate football game, between Rutgers and Princeton in 1869. In the next fifty years, it was known for its gutsy little teams—often beaten but always game.

▼
The first football game, held on 6 November 1869, was played in a field on the site of the present gym on College Avenue. Rutgers won, 6—4. The game was more like soccer than like modern American football. Twenty-five men from each side played; students liked early football because "everyone" could participate. This re-creation of the game, by William M. Boyd '32, is the most charming of a number of such generally inaccurate attempts. The postures of the figures suggest the freeze-action poses people had to adopt in late-nineteenth-century "action" photography.

▶
An 1888 student sketch of the game, suggesting its rugbylike qualities at the time.

▼
The Rutgers varsity football team in a studio photo, 1881. Rule changes in the direction of British rugby had been adopted in the 1870s, but the uniquely American line of scrimmage had been adopted as well, and the teams had been reduced to eleven players. There were no professional coaches until the early twentieth century; late-nineteenth-century intercollegiate football was entirely student-run. The uniforms look too tidy to be actual game wear. The pre-forward-pass ball is rounder than today's, and the players wear no helmets or other protective gear.

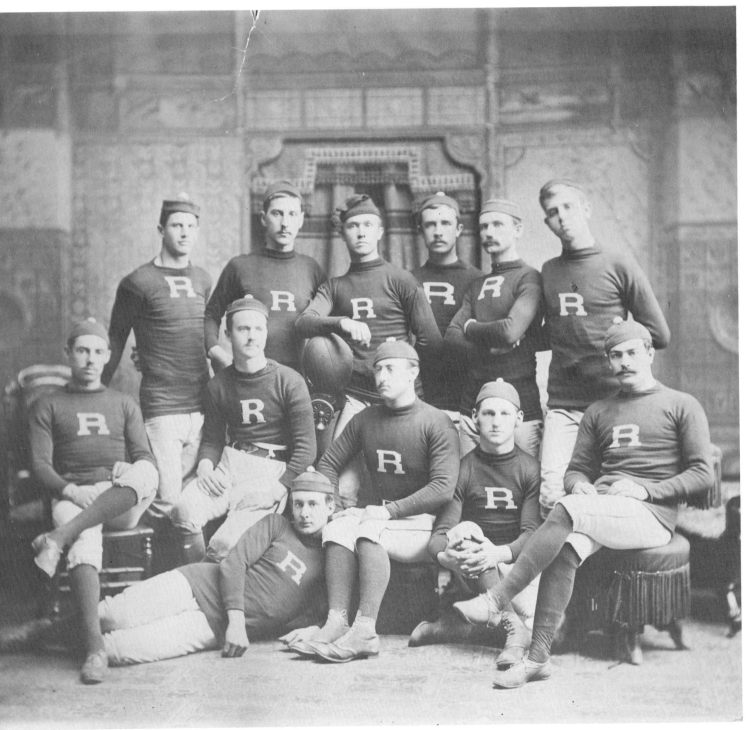

► William Van Dyke, the first Rutgers football "coach" and Rutgers' oldest living alumnus in 1980.

▼ This wonderful photo is probably of the Rutgers varsity and its student supporters. The youth holding the ball is the same William Van Dyke pictured above, here captain of the 1894–1895 squad. After he graduated, he volunteered his services as coach for a year or two, on a part-time basis. The 1894 team won four games and lost six. The photo is unusual in apparently showing the team bloodied up after a game; compare the clothes to those in the 1881 formal picture (opposite). The banner probably belongs to the class of '95, whose members were the "backbone" of the '94 varsity (the members of the '95 football team had been so good during their freshman and sophomore years that by their junior and senior years no other class team would play against them). The significance of the dress of the supporters in the upper left is not known. The dog is Delta Phi's "Duncan."

Listen ! If the wise man of to-day were to study for one hundred years trying to invent a game which would give more healthy exercise, courage, generalship and ambition, and be more popular with the college student than that of "foot-ball," his labors would result in a miserable failure; and you agree with me, too. But whoever saw a vigorous game which had no risks about it and no chances of being hurt? If there is one, the girls monopolize it.

As you see in the above, accidents are liable to occur, and it is sensible to have a reliable and efficient remedy close at hand, during all games, such as RENNE'S PAIN-KILLING MAGIC OIL. It is a sovereign lotion for all bruises, sprains, cuts, contusions, colic, rheumatism and diarrhœa. Try it. Sold everywhere.

▶ By the 1890s football was well-established as an American symbol of manliness. Advertisers were also beginning to focus on a specifically collegiate market. An ad from the 1893 yearbook.

▶ Removing the rocks from Neilson Field, the old football field near the present site of Alexander Library, probably in the early 1890s. Late-nineteenth-century students often complained (or bragged) about their rocky playing fields and about the sticky red mud of New Brunswick.

▼
The 1903 varsity. The padded leggings are warm-ups, not for games; the ball looks a little sleeker. The young men in coats and ties at either end of the back row are the student coaches.

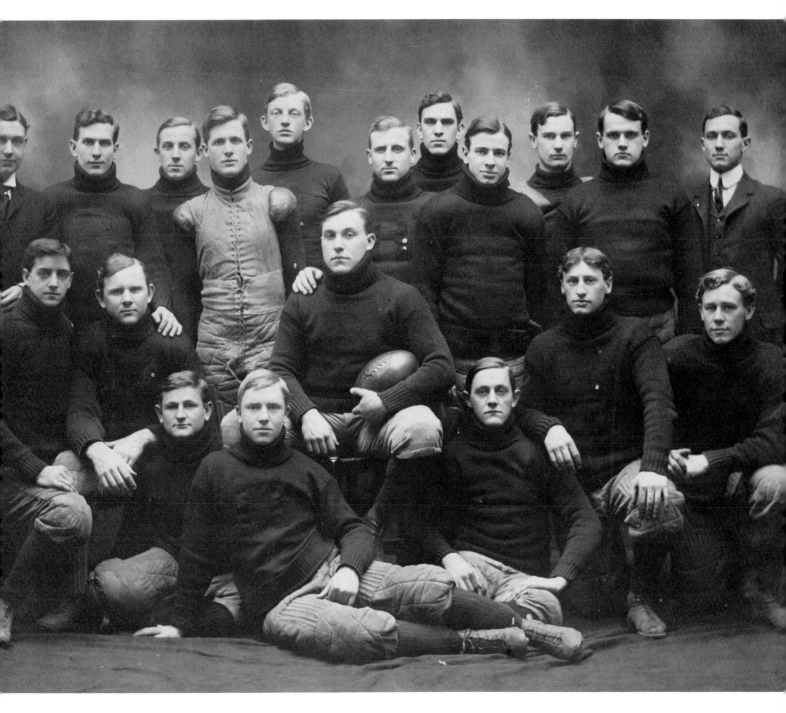

About 1905 there was considerable national concern about the violence of collegiate football. Teddy Roosevelt (of all people) threatened to outlaw the game unless it was cleaned up. Extensive rule changes followed, forbidding such dangerous formations as the flying wedge, legalizing the forward pass, and mandating protective gear. This 1906 Rutgers varsity photo shows the result—adoption of the old leather helmet and shoulder pads.

▶
Philip M. Brett, captain of the 1891 Rutgers football team, later trustee and acting president of Rutgers, had the slogan "I'd die for dear old Rutgers" incorrectly attributed to him. According to a later recollection, "Brett confided . . . that his life had been a burden ever since and that he was one with Job. At least once a week he had to steel himself to the greeting: 'Hello, Phil, old man; dying for dear old Rutgers these days?'" Perhaps this had something to do with his unwillingness in the early 1930s to accept a permanent appointment as Rutgers' president. A drawing from a New York newspaper, 1929.

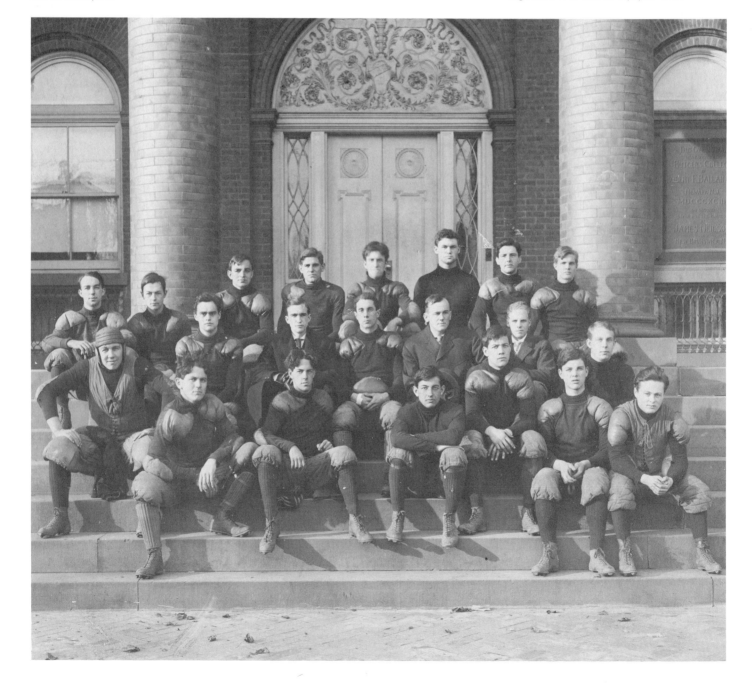

A FOOTBALL CAPTAIN WHO BECAME A COLLEGE PRESIDENT

BRETT WAS LONG BELIEVED TO BE THE ORIGINAL MAN WHO'D "DIE FOR DEAR OLD RUTGERS" — BUT FACTS NOW PROVE THE CLASSIC PHRASE WAS UTTERED BY "POP" GRANT IN THE 1892 PRINCETON-RUTGERS GAME!

BRETT LED HIS 1891 RUTGERS TEAM TO FAME BY HOLDING THE POWERFUL PRINCETON TEAM OF THAT YEAR TO A 12 TO 0 VICTORY!

NOW HE IS A CORPORATION LAWYER IN NEW YORK, AS WELL AS ACTING PRESIDENT OF RUTGERS — SINCE THE RESIGNATION OF DR. JOHN THOMAS.

GUS UNIMON

PHILIP MILLEDOLER BRETT, CLASS 1892 New York City.
Born at Newark, N. J., Feb. 17, 1871. Lawyer. Lieutenant, National Guard N. J., 1903–08. Trustee, Rutgers, 1906– . LL.B. (N. Y. Law School, 1894).

OTHER SPORTS

Other sports besides football were popular at late-nineteenth-century Rutgers.

▶ The track team, 1894, featuring one of the new bicycles—and some especially splendid mustaches.

▼ The varsity baseball team, 1890, on the side steps of Kirkpatrick. The catcher's mask and chest pad are the first pieces of protective equipment to appear in any Rutgers sports shot; the first primitive little baseball mitts do not appear for another five or ten years.

▼
The fencing team, early twentieth century.

On the Banks

Rutgers students expressed their college spirit by writing many Rutgers songs from about 1870 to about 1910. They were often rewrites of older songs.

▶

An early version of "On the Banks of the Old Raritan," by Howard Fuller '74—virtually the college anthem in later years. Based on "On the Banks of the Old Dundee," this version is from the first songbook, published by the students in 1885. Other songs at this time included "Bow-wow-wow!" based on the old Rutgers football cheer; "Poco's Daughter," about a blighted love affair between an undergraduate and the daughter of a pawnbroker who lived on Burnet Street; "Vive les Rutgers Sons"; and the "Rutgers Foot-Ball Song":

Oh, we'll kick her over, or rip the cover,
No help for the fellows that fall,
They must take their show for a bruise or two
Who follow the bully foot-ball.

ON THE BANKS OF THE OLD RARITAN.

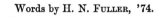

Words by H. N. FULLER, '74.

2 As Fresh, they used me rather roughly,
　But I the fearful gauntlet ran,
　　And they shook me so about
　　That they turned me inside out,
　On the banks of the old Raritan.

3 I passed through all these tortures nobly,
　And then, as Soph, my turn began,
　　And I hazed the poor Fresh so
　　That they longed for Heaven, I know,
　On the banks of the old Raritan.

4 And then I rested at my pleasure,
　And steered quite clear of Prex's ban,
　　And the stars their good-bye kissing

　　Found me not from euchre missing,
　On the banks of the old Raritan.

5 And soon I made my social *entrée*,
　When I laid full many a wicked plan,
　　And by my cunning art
　　Slew many a maiden's heart,
　On the banks of the old Raritan

6 Then sing aloud to Alma Mater,
　And keep the Scarlet in the van;
　　For with her motto high
　　Rutgers' name shall never die,
　On the banks of the old Raritan.

Albany, N.Y., April 4, 1914.

Dr. W.H.S. Demarest,

President of Rutgers College,

    New Brunswick, N.J.

Dear Mr. President:

    I have written three verses for our old college song, and a revised transcript of the whole song to revised form appears below, which I place in your hands with misgiving, yet with the devout [hope] that it may prove a true [and] satisfactory medium for the [fluent] expression of those staunch and [stead]y and fervent feelings of love and [loya]lty which every reverent son of [Rutg]ers must needs have in his heart [for] his "gracious Alma Mater."

On the Banks of the Old Raritan.

[M]y father sent me to old Rutgers,
[An]d resolved that I should be a man;
And so I settled down,
In that noisy college town,
[O]n the banks of the old Raritan.

Chorus: On the banks of the old Raritan, my boys,
Where old Rutgers evermore shall stand;
For has she not stood,
Since the time of the flood,
On the banks of the old Raritan.

Her ardent spirit stirred and cheered me,
From the day my college years began,
Gracious Alma Mater mine;
Learning's fair and honored shrine;
On the banks of the old Raritan.

I love her flaming, far-flung banner,
I love her triumphs proud to scan,
And I glory in the fame
That's immortalized her name,
On the banks of the old Raritan.

My heart clings closer than the ivy-
As life runs out its fleeting span
To the stately, ancient walls
Of her hallowed, classic halls,
On the banks of the old Raritan.

Then sing aloud to Alma Mater,
And keep the Scarlet in the van;
For with her motto high,
Rutgers' name shall never die,
On the banks of the old Raritan.

Faithfully yours,
Howard N. Fuller

▲ In 1914 Fuller, then 63, wrote to President Demarest of Rutgers submitting a new version of "On the Banks"—which was adopted. It removed the possibly undignified references of the earlier version to rushing and hazing.

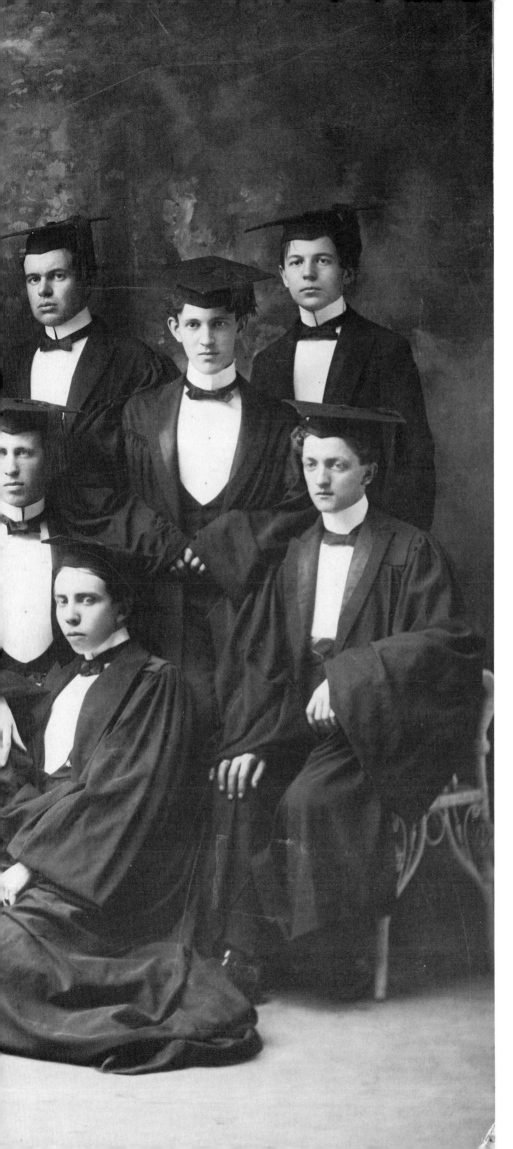

◄
GLEE CLUB
The Glee Club started as an informal singing group reorganized every year; it began singing the songs of college loyalty at the same time that intercollegiate sports developed—in the 1870s. Like intercollegiate sports, it was entirely student-run until the early twentieth century, when college authorities took it over. In this 1890 photograph, members of the Glee Club have initiated the revival of the old scholars' dress worn by everyone in the early-nineteenth-century college. In the early twentieth century, the seniors briefly experimented with it as their class uniform but found it too uncomfortable. It then settled in as graduation apparel.

THEATRICALS

In the 1880s, student theatricals became popular, with the performance of a number of plays written by students in the 1890s, including one mocking late-nineteenth-century feminism and the coeducation movement—"The Triple Alliance: College Life Ten Years Hence (Coeducation at Rutgers)."

► This photo is a meeting of the "dramatic club" at the "George H. Cook house." Two of the young ladies who evidently acted with the students were Cook's daughters, Emma (sitting on the ground, left) and Anna (sitting in the chair, right).

Another theatrical group, more elaborately posed in one of the settings favored by professional photographers, 1890.

AND BY OUR CUNNING ART —— SLEW WE MANY A MAIDEN HEART. ON THE BANKS OF THE OLD RARITAN.

TAKEN FROM :86 :87: JUNE 1885.

PHOTO-ENG.CO. N.Y.

STUDENT ROMANCE

We may think of Victorian Americans as straitlaced, but nineteenth-century Rutgers students saw themselves as Don Juans. In 1898, a Rutgers undergraduate from a respectable New Brunswick family was accused by his grandfather of "pay[ing] too close attention to some young girls whose acquaintance he could not afford to cultivate intimately." When his family did not believe his protestations of innocence, he went up to his room and shot himself. Kirkpatrick Chapel contains a stained-glass window in his memory, on which is one of the few verses associated with Rutgers that is actually good poetry, appropriately from *Adonais*, Shelley's elegy on the death of Keats:

He has outsoared the shadow of our night;
Envy and calumny and hate and pain,
And that unrest which men miscall delight
Can touch him not and torture not again.

This celebration of collegiate romantic prowess is from the 1887 yearbook.

BANQUETS AND DANCES
In the 1890s the classes added new customs to their yearly round of ceremonies: class banquets and class dances. The rivalries acted out in the older exhibitions and rushes were transferred to the banquets. At least once, a rival class arrived early, locked the doors, and ate the other's banquet. More commonly, the rival class tried to kidnap the banqueting class's president.

▼
Menu for a class banquet, 1901.

◄
The Sophomore Hop, 1904.

Second Annual Banquet of the Class of 1903.

HELD AT THE MANSION HOUSE.

JANUARY 3, 1901.

....

Menu.

BLUE POINTS.

CONSOMME AU TAPIOCA.

CELERY.   QUEEN OLIVES.   RADISHES.

CHICKEN.   HALIBUT, A LA HOLLANDAISE.

POTATOES CHATEAU.

SMALL PATTIES, A LA TOULOUSE.

FRENCH PEAS.

PUNCH, A LA 1903.

ROAST PHILADELPHIA SQUAB ON TOAST.

LETTUCE AND TOMATOE SALADE.

CREAM PUFFS, A LA MANSION HOUSE.

FANCY ICE CREAM.

PETIT FOURS.   LADIES' FINGERS.

ASSORTED CAKES.   ORANGES.   BON BONS.

AFRICAN BARS.   MACAROONS.

COFFEE.

▼
PROM, 1913
This photo of the 1913 prom was apparently not posed. It was taken with strong interior lighting in the old Ballantine Gym.

STUDENT CADETS
Student military training was organized after the Civil War but did not become really popular until the 1890s.

▶ In 1900 the cadets were still wearing Civil War–vintage uniforms.

▼
When this impressive panorama of the Rutgers cadet corps was taken in the early twentieth century, both horse-drawn carriages and early automobiles were in use. (Only the first three panels are shown here.) A panorama like this was photographed with a special camera that swept in a semicircle; the apparent straight line of cadets in fact stood in a semicircle around it. The camera was centered somewhere near the present site of Van Dyke Hall on the College Avenue Campus. Hertzog Hall is on the left; Milledoler is in the center, with a Johnson & Johnson stack behind it; Murray is slanting off to its right; and the building on the right, now torn down, was yet another house in which George H. Cook once lived. The curving street is the old Bleecker Mall, now a line of trees and a lawn (the statue of William the Silent presently stands near its left end).

Corps of Cadets-Rutger College-1912-13

STUDENT ROOMS

The first photographs of the interiors of student rooms were snapshots by the students themselves; snapshot photography became widespread only after 1900. Students had gloried in their funky bachelor rooms for many years. In 1870, an anonymous *Targum* correspondent wrote of his boardinghouse room:

My room is the "second story, back," in a modest looking frame building . . . the window can be used as a door, especially very early in the morning . . . the key makes an excellent implement to crack nuts with . . . I am proud of my library . . . Byron . . . Tennyson . . . Graeca Majora: [a] book flask has been there for three years . . . the students of Rutgers College are fond of Greek—a long way off . . . as soon as an article is deemed unworthy to occupy a conspicuous place in the room it is consigned to oblivion by being thrown under the bed . . . I sometimes allow a visitor to creep under . . . and enjoy himself for an hour or two.

▼

A matey group of students around 1900. After this time, students rarely posed with their arms around one another. Twentieth-century male sensibilities apparently found the posture too compromising.

▶
ALUMNI
After 1910 the college began to cultivate alumni support more carefully. All the alumni up to the class of 1916 were listed in the general catalog published on the occasion of Rutgers' 150th anniversary; in 1914, the *Rutgers Alumni Quarterly* (later the *Rutgers Alumni Magazine*) began publication. The photo of this alumni association dinner at the Hotel Astor, New York, 1914, was taken with a *banquet camera*.

▼
A fraternity house interior (DKE), 1915.

ANNUAL DINNER
OF
THE RUTGERS COLLEGE ALUMNI ASS'N.
OF
THE CITY OF NEW YORK.

HOTEL ASTOR   JAN. 16. 1914.

▶
GARRET A. HOBART

In 1950 Richard P. McCormick calculated that
there were about two dozen colleges with more
alumni in the *Dictionary of American Biography*
than Rutgers—not a bad record considering the
small size of Rutgers through most of the nineteenth century. Eminent nineteenth-century
alumni included four governors of New Jersey;
U.S. Supreme Court Justice Joseph P. Bradley
'36, who cast the deciding vote in the disputed
Hayes-Tilden presidential election in 1876; Civil
War General George H. Sharp '47; the mathe-
matician George William Hill '59; the railroad
magnate Lenore F. Loree '77; and Garret A.
Hobart '63, in whom Rutgers came within
a heartbeat of having an alumnus as president
of the United States. As an undergraduate at
Rutgers, Hobart took honors in mathematics and
English, and lived in the rowdy Mansion House
downtown (though his peers remember him as
unmischievous). After graduation he became a
wealthy corporate leader and a skilled political
manipulator. McKinley chose him as his vice-
president in 1892 because he was sound on gold
and counteracted the easy-money Democrats.
Though he was not known as an orator, he got
off one quotable line in his acceptance speech:
"An honest dollar, worth one hundred cents
everywhere, cannot be coined out of fifty-three
cents of silver plus a legislative fiat." He died in
office before McKinley's assassination and was
replaced by Teddy Roosevelt.

IN THE PUBLIC EYE.

Garrett A. Hobart.

From a photograph—Copyright, 1896, by Davis & Sanford, New York.

▼
150TH ANNIVERSARY, 1916
The sesquicentennial celebration of the founding of the college included elaborate pageantry. This scene is said to be a reenactment of the crossing of the Raritan River by the Dutch in 1730; they are about to be welcomed with open arms by the English already settled in New Brunswick.

1929

1926

1931

1837

Rutge
Harv
18

1940

1914

First Greek Letter
Fraternity ~ 1845

1940

1927

1910

gers
eats
ceton
69

1908

1922

1845

1889

1809

1941

1870

1903

Sign of the
Red Lion Tave
1771

1841

1865

1872

annon War ~ 1875

1766 Q 19

October 1941

"Where State and Ivy Meet" 1916–1945

Up to World War I, Rutgers was one faculty and one campus—a college with a nineteenth-century reputation like those of the other old Eastern, mostly private schools that would be labeled the Ivy League by a sportswriter in the 1930s. But this simplicity and this image did not last much longer. In the 1880s, the Rutgers faculty had recommended coeducation, but the trustees had quickly said No, with loud student approval. Around 1910 the New Jersey State Federation of Women's Clubs began to raise the issue again; the spokeswoman was Mabel Smith Douglass, an activist from Jersey City and a Barnard graduate. Once more, Rutgers said No—claiming that its "traditional" identity would be jeopardized—but President Demarest indicated that the college would not reject the idea of a "parallel, coordinate, women's college." Two of Demarest's opponents on the Board of Trustees, James Neilson and Lenore Loree (both of whom were in favor of Rutgers having much closer ties to the state) backed Douglass, and in 1918 the women's college opened with Douglass as dean, using as quarters two homes on what is now the Douglass Campus, Carpender and Cooper. To emphasize state service, the new college was called New Jersey College for Women, NJC for short. Remarkably quickly, NJC established itself as a quality liberal arts college, emphasizing the subjects educated young ladies were expected to be good at in the 1920s: the arts, languages, education, and home economics. NJC was loosely linked to Rutgers—technically subordinate but in fact enjoying considerable autonomy—and in 1924 Rutgers for the first time formally adopted the name Rutgers University. Rutgers College also formally disappeared at this time, and its student body was reorganized into degree-granting abstractions of faculty and curricula: arts and sciences, engineering, agriculture, education, ceramics, and chemistry.

At the same time, the Agricultural Experiment Station, which had been running extension education and "short courses" off and on for a number of years, was strongly encouraged by the state to improve its agricultural education for undergraduates, and in 1914 the College of Agriculture was organized. Four new buildings were put up on the present Cook Campus between 1914 and 1922, but not until the 1970s were there dormitories at the old College Farm; most agricultural students at Rutgers, virtually all men, lived and studied certain subjects on the College Avenue Campus, and initiated what is today a basic feature of undergraduate life at Rutgers—regular migration across town for classes (the campus buses were a long way in the future, however).

In the 1920s, a time of economic boom in the United States, Rutgers and NJC expanded rapidly. More dorms were built at Rutgers in the late 1920s, and academic buildings and a chapel at NJC. By 1929 the university, which had had 641 students in 1920, enrolled 1,401 in the "men's colleges" and 1,159 at NJC—2,660 students in all (not counting a few graduate students and one or two other special categories). In 1927 the first extra–New Brunswick addition to Rutgers was built, the School of Pharmacy in Newark, founded privately in 1894. The 1920s also saw two institutional events not unfamiliar today: Rutgers' first "reorganization"—the

◄
COLLEGE AVENUE MAP, 1941
Map of the College Avenue Campus, 1941, including building dates and now legendary Rutgers events.

creation of a university-wide administrative structure and an attempt to introduce businesslike efficiency and cost accounting into higher education (also Loree's doing)—and an unfortunately failed plan to centralize geographically where there was enough space for the university to grow as a single unit, on what is today the Douglass-Cook Campus. The plan was killed when the state put Route 1 right through the center of the proposed unified campus; the fact that Rutgers was unable to lobby against this action indicates how poor its political connections with the state were during that period.

In this new, increasingly complex university, student life changed considerably. Academic life was considerably harder than it had been in the nineteenth century, probably due to the increasing professionalism of the faculty, and it was no longer so easy to get through the college. Up to one-third of the incoming class did not make it through their freshman years, and the average grade, which had been as high as 90 in the late nineteenth century, dropped to about 77 in the 1920s. The curriculum was much larger and more diverse, and it had been organized and standardized in ways that would make a student from the 1920s more at home in modern Rutgers than in the Rutgers of the 1890s, when the only choice had been between two relatively inflexible schools—"classical" and "scientific." The faculty was organized into fifteen departments by 1929, most of them familiar today—though in somewhat different proportions. Agriculture was the largest department, with 31 faculty members, followed by language (17) and engineering (14). Economics was growing fast (10); history was combined with political science (10); one eclectic department was called psychology, art, and music (and also included a sociologist) (10); and the physics department had only 3 members. Students were much less likely to know all the faculty members personally than they had been in the late nineteenth century, though the atmosphere was a long way from the impersonality of the present university. Most of the faculty still lived in town; many were well known, influential personalities to the students; and the faculty was still composed basically of undergraduate educators whose fundamental loyalties were expected to go to Rutgers. Tenure was some distance in the future; research was still unmentioned in the description of a faculty member's duties; and only 50 of the 160 faculty members at Rutgers in 1929 held Ph.D.s.

As much as they could, the students went on living their own lives independent of adult concerns. The 1920s were also a boom time for youth, the era of the flapper and the speakeasy—the Jazz Age—and Rutgers students participated as fully as they could. The Glee Club began to tour with a band called the Rutgers Jazz Bandits, and a few student musicians from that era went on to professional careers. The most famous was Ozzie Nelson '27. Relations between young men and women were much freer in the 1920s than they had been before World War I, and with eligible young women available for the first time in large numbers at NJC (they were then called Coopies after their main dorm, Cooper), "social life" became a salient part of student culture for the first time, although the chaperone was still a fixture at any kind of mixed event. On one occasion in the 1920s, some NJC women caught in a speakeasy with Rutgers students in downtown New Brunswick tried unsuccessfully to bluff their way out of the fix with their dean by claiming they had been doing sociological research there. The fraternities flourished, as the center of both social life and campus politics; elections for student offices were often determined by voting alliances, or "combines," between the fraternities, with the poor "independents"—déclassé nonfraternity men—left out in the cold. The fraternities, like the older literary societies, were also serious socializing institutions; an alumnus from the late 1930s remembers the strict dress code and etiquette in his house, and the well-attended weekly meetings run by parliamentary procedure. The golden age of Rutgers football began in 1913, when the first real coach, Foster Sanford, came to Rutgers; he cannot quite be called a professional, since he donated his services. Especially memorable were two all-Americans and two almost undefeated teams: Paul Robeson in the 1917–1918 season and Homer Hazel in 1923–1924. Student clubs and other activities also flourished in the 1920s, with increasing numbers of preprofessional groups.

The biggest change in student life at Rutgers in the 1920s came as the expanding university redefined its obligations to the students and invented new mechanisms for controlling them. As at other colleges at the time, Rutgers was discovering the "well-rounded student." "Our objective in education," President Clothier said in 1930, "is not the development of men and women of high intellectuality alone, but men and women who are well-balanced." Late-nineteenth-century students had had the same view; the extracurriculum was as important to them as the curriculum. Late-nineteenth-century students had developed the extracurriculum themselves, however; now the college was taking it over, much as American colleges had taken over the intellectual innovations of the early-nineteenth-century student literary societies with their late-nineteenth-century curricular reforms. And to do so, college authorities had to reduce still further the effective autonomy that the students had possessed in the late nineteenth century.

In the mid-1920s Rutgers hired Fraser Metzger as its third dean of students, now called the dean of men; NJC had a separate dean of women with the same functions. Metzger instituted the first comprehensive student-life program in the history of the college. Class warfare, the means by which Rutgers students had fostered their class and college spirit since the 1860s, had been declining in the 1920s, probably a casualty of the increasing diversity of the students and size of the classes. Metzger reorganized dorm life into freshman dorms and upperclass dorms, on the theory that class spirit would develop naturally if the classes simply lived together. He installed housemothers and preceptors (selected undergraduate authorities) in the dorms; sometime later housemothers were placed in the fraternities. He further developed academic advising and elaborated freshman orientation (testing had been inaugurated after World War I). The college began monitoring most other student activities at the time and eliminated the last traces of student management of athletics. And a new student-activities fee was levied to make the students help pay for all of this.

These changes were not one hundred percent effective, and they by no means affected the ability of students to find subtle and imaginative ways to circumvent adult authority in the college. Fraternities seem to have remained particularly impervious to control—a reason, perhaps, for their continuing importance during the difficult Depression years to come. But with the changes, the students lost most of the remaining responsibility that they had held, not always with the most mature of results, in the autonomous days of the nineteenth century. Certainly it is hard to imagine the growing university managing its students with the laissez-faire methods of the nineteenth century; but about the time the student life authorities took over, much of the creativity and vitality went out of campus life at Rutgers, and a passivity characteristic of the modern college student, broken by regular "activist" interludes, became more common. Students still had fun in college, but the alumni of the 1930s and later do not seem to remember college life with the same enthusiasm as the alumni of earlier years. What the older alumni were remembering, it seems, was the thrill of freedom and initiative.

Rutgers' postwar expansion ended abruptly with the onset of the Great Depression in the 1930s. The new state funding of the 1920s dried up, and the combined enrollments of Rutgers and NJC dropped by 600. At one point in the early 1930s, the dorms at Rutgers were running 40 percent vacant, a warning to later administrators not to build new dorms too quickly. Faculty salaries were cut back, no new faculty members were hired for ten years, and such vocational courses as business became much more popular among the students, much as they have in the recessions of the late 1970s and early 1980s.

Unlike the present, however, the 1930s also saw notable political activities among the students: the founding of the Liberal Club and of a socially conscious lecture series in the early 1930s; an antiwar movement attacking on-campus ROTC, and a powerful antifraternity movement organized by a group called the Scarlet Barbarians in the mid-1930s. At Rutgers as elsewhere, if the fun and games of the late nineteenth century had been the first example of a distinctive "adolescent" stage of life in America, the 1930s saw the first significant example of "postadolescent" behavior, when college students applied themselves to more serious collegiate and societal issues. The activism of the 1930s was considerably less thorough and disruptive than that of the 1960s, but as in the 1960s, it did result in reaction by adults connected with the university. In 1939, for example, the alumni counterattacked the antifraternity movement in the pages of the *Rutgers Alumni Magazine*, and the fraternities recovered their political hegemony within the college for a short time.

Conventional college life went on at Rutgers during the 1930s, with adaptations to the hard times. After World War I, increasing numbers of Rutgers students had worked their way through college. Now, more students lived at home and commuted to college. The fraternities dug in and survived; "anyone who was anyone" was in them, according to the reminiscences of a late-1930s fraternity member. Nonfraternal groups took on fraternal guise: Raritan House at the College Avenue Campus; Alpha Phalpha at the agricultural college, an economical student-cooperative living arrangement in some houses on the College Farm that had been bought up cheaply during the Depression. Like other American institutions that were able to keep going during the Depression, the university generally benefited from low land prices; it was during this period that much of the land that is now the Busch Campus was acquired, and the stadium was built with WPA help in the mid-1930s. In 1938 the Rutgers football team inaugurated the new stadium by beating Princeton for the first time since the original football game in 1869, by the squeaker score of 20 to 18—perhaps the most memorable single event of the decade for many alumni.

Though the college remained poor and underenrolled in the late 1930s, it was not without its strong points. A fair amount of scholarship money was available; as today, Rutgers was a good place to get a decent education inexpensively. It was no longer so tightly integrated and personalistic as the late-nineteenth-century college, but graduates of the late 1930s do still remember it as a community in ways that it is not today—as a small and friendly place where freshmen were taught to say hello to everyone and where you knew all the members of your class, even if you no longer met with them collectively or hazed the lower classes with much spirit. Noncommuting students in earlier years were kept on campus through the weekends by college regulations; by the 1930s these rules had disappeared, but the same end was accomplished by the lack of students' cars—the last time in Rutgers' history that the college was not a "suitcase campus." As a result, campuswide activities were better supported than they are today—dances, clubs, athletics, concerts, and lecture series. NJC had much the same character and probably kept it longer after World War II than did the men's college.

By the late 1930s Rutgers' Ivy League–like identity was probably a thing of the past, at least to the locals. A late-1930s alumnus remembers that schools like Lafayette looked down on Rutgers. Due to the weakness of its original denominational base, and due to what can only be called an uninspired line of college and university presidents, Rutgers simply had not established itself as a thriving private institution. What institutional successes it had had in the 1920s were linked to the state and to the actions of a few vigorous trustees; this basis for institutional vigor had been killed by the Depression. A doggerel line in the alumni magazine in the late 1940s asked rhetorically if Rutgers was "standing with reluctant feet where State and Ivy Meet." As the nation went through a major change from noninvolvement to total commitment in the international events that led to World War II, this is precisely what the college and university continued to do.

▶
COLLEGE AVENUE CAMPUS, 1931
An aerial view of the College Avenue Campus, taken about 1931 (the College Avenue Gym is still going up (upper left) after the Ballantine Gym fire). This is an unusually striking photo due to the angle of the shadows and the long focal length of the camera. Rutgers had no real traffic problem by modern standards—though this photo was taken fairly early in the day. The area behind Murray Hall that is now a big parking lot (center right) was apparently just some grass on which the cars pulled up.

▼
COLLEGE AVENUE, 1937
The last building on the left side of the first block is Rutgers University Press, founded in 1937, occupying quarters that were formerly a boardinghouse, and where it remains today. The midday streets are filled with parked cars, but the university still felt no need to construct parking lots.

▼
New Brunswick, 1924
In 1924 downtown New Brunswick still had trolley tracks. The city remained a prosperous
manufacturing center and did not really start to
deteriorate until the wave of American subur-
banization after World War II. This is a view from
the corner of Albany and George streets toward
Rutgers College, of which only the Old Queen's
cupola is visible.

University Organization in the Early Twentieth Century
The nineteenth-century college had consisted of faculty, students, and trustees. As the twentieth-century university grew, it became more complex and diverse, and a new controlling entity emerged—the administration.

▶
In 1926 there were 21 administrators at Rutgers (the president, 6 deans, and 14 others including the treasurer, the librarian, and the head of buildings and grounds), managing 140 faculty members and a little over 1,000 students (including those at NJC). As today, many of the administrative functions were relatively invisible or abstract from the student point of view, but one was not: the original deans' function of judging student conduct.

▶▶
The organization of the university, 1932. The residential male students for all these colleges lived on the Rutgers College Campus, and the women on the campus of the New Jersey College for Women. Pharmacy was in Newark, without a campus. The only significant number—in the dozens—of graduate students were in the College of Agriculture.

ADMINISTRATION

Rutgers University

1766—Chartered as Queen's College by George III.

1825—Name changed to Rutgers College.

1864—Constituted the Land Grant College of New Jersey.

1917—Designated The State University of New Jersey by Act of Legislature.

1924—Trustees adopted Rutgers University as title of the entire institution.

THE COLLEGE OF ARTS AND SCIENCES.   Walter T. Marvin, Dean
    Courses in Liberal Arts, Business Administration, Journalism, Chemistry
    and Biology. Also courses preparatory to Medicine, Law and Theology.

THE COLLEGE OF ENGINEERING.   Parker H. Daggett, Dean
    Courses in Civil, Electrical, Mechanical, Municipal and Sanitary, and
    Industrial Engineering.

THE COLLEGE OF AGRICULTURE.   Jacob G. Lipman, Dean
    Courses in General Agriculture, Preparation for Research, Dairying,
    Pomology, Vegetable Production, Poultry Husbandry, Floriculture, Land-
    scape Gardening.

THE SCHOOL OF EDUCATION.   Charles H. Elliott, Dean
    Courses preparatory to Teaching and School Supervision.

THE DEPARTMENT OF CERAMICS.   George H. Brown, Dean
    Courses in Ceramics.

THE NEW JERSEY COLLEGE FOR WOMEN.   Mabel S. Douglass, Dean
    Courses in Liberal Arts, General Science and Home Economics.

THE NEW JERSEY COLLEGE OF PHARMACY.   Ernest Little, Dean
    Three-year course in Pharmacy.

For catalog of the College for Men apply to
LUTHER H. MARTIN

For catalog of the New Jersey College for Women apply to
ESTHER WARE HAWES

▲
LENORE LOREE
Lenore Loree graduated from Rutgers in 1877 and became a wealthy railway magnate. As a Rutgers trustee in the early twentieth century, he was a real mover and shaker, more influential than any of the presidents of the university during the same period. He brought the great football coach Foster Sanford to Rutgers in 1913 (Sanford had coached Loree's son at Yale), he badgered the university with his businessman's ideas of efficiency in the 1920s, and he was, along with James Neilson, the key supporter of the New Jersey College for Women. An example of his style: Antilles Field was donated to NJC by Neilson and Loree in 1922, named after the ship *Antilles*, which Loree had chartered in 1914 to bring American expatriates back from Europe. In 1917, the ship was torpedoed and sunk. For the christening of the field, Loree arranged for a visit by the American airship *Shenandoah*, which the navy then flew out of Lakehurst; the visit had to be canceled at the last minute due to bad weather. Given the record of early-twentieth-century American lighter-than-air ships in bad weather, it was probably just as well.

TO JOHNNY THOMAS

————

Who works away from morn till night?
Who keeps the flagstones clean and bright?
Who tends the Hall and lights the light?
Johnny Thomas.

Who cuts the grass and rakes the leaves?
Who trims and sprays the campus trees?
Who does whatever work he sees?
Johnny Thomas.

Who shovels paths amid the snow?
Who makes the furnace fires go?
Who makes the campus flowers grow?
Johnny Thomas.

Who knows what all our teams can do?
Who knows professors, old and new?
Who knows old Rutgers through and through?
Johnny Thomas.

Who knows each fellow at the Dorm.,
And meets him with a greeting warm?
Well known to us his portly form:
Johnny Thomas.

Who, when all his work is done,
Should have his portrait stately hung
Trustees and Presidents among?
Johnny Thomas.

◀
THE JANITOR
The janitor was the first nonfaculty employee of the college, predating any administrators or secretaries by at least half a century. In the nineteenth century, there was only one janitor to do everything—caring for the buildings and grounds and such other duties as subduing rowdy students and leading the Commencement procession (a not entirely honorific position, since when the assemblage arrived at the church, it entered back to front, so the janitor was last in, just after the freshmen). The janitorial role, like others at Rutgers, was often hereditary. Johnny Thomas (in this picture from a 1915 student scrapbook) was the son of a nineteenth-century janitor; and the son of the night watchman in 1915, "General" Cox is, in 1984, retired from Rutgers Buildings and Grounds. Like everything else at Rutgers, the maintenance staff has expanded exponentially in the twentieth-century university. In 1984 Rutgers (including Newark and Camden) employed 1,067 "service" and "maintenance" personnel, and 294 "skilled craftsmen." Judging from the frequent complaints about the dirtiness of the college in the nineteenth-century faculty minutes, the place is probably a good deal cleaner and tidier than it once was.

▶
WILLIAM H. S. DEMAREST, 1907
William H. S. Demarest was the only Rutgers alumnus ever to serve as president of the college. He graduated in the class of 1883, a member of the fourth generation of his family to be connected with Rutgers, and served as president from 1906 until 1924, when he stepped down due to policy disagreements with some of the trustees. He lived into his nineties (more than one president lived a long and pleasant life after resigning from Rutgers), and died in 1956. Demarest also wrote the first history of the college, published in 1924.

◄◄
MABEL SMITH DOUGLASS
Mabel Smith Douglass was a Barnard-educated woman active in the New Jersey State Federation of Women's Clubs' campaign which lobbied against the state's lax attitude toward coeducation. She was the founding dean of the New Jersey College for Women (which was renamed in her honor in 1955) from 1918 until 1930—an energetic woman who, in alliance with Loree and Neilson, got the college off the ground with remarkable speed.

COLLEGE HALL, NJC
The old Carpender estate, now College Hall, is as central to the iconography of Douglass College as Old Queen's is to Rutgers. And like Old Queen's, it was the original, all-purpose building (though not for as long)—classrooms, dean's apartment, lab, dorm, chapel, even gym.

◄
College Hall today.

▼
A twentieth-century drawing based on an old print of College Hall as a private home, in the mid-nineteenth century.

▶
Packing-crate Gym
In its early years, New Jersey College for Women had to struggle for accommodations. The "packing-crate gym," built out of unused military crates from World War I, was located between the later site of Voorhees Chapel and the ravine. In 1918, when this picture was taken, it was briefly used as a dorm. Then it served for more than forty years as a gym, until the construction of Loree Gymnasium.

COOPER HALL

Cooper was one of the two original buildings at NJC and had been the home of Professor Jacob Cooper, professor of Greek at Rutgers from 1866 to 1904. It was on the corner of George and Nicol (now a lawn). When the college was founded, Mrs. Douglass was told she could rent it if she could convince its lodgers to move out; they were bachelor professors at the agricultural school. After a war of nerves lasting a few months, they agreed to leave. The building served over the years—with numerous additions—as a dorm, a dining hall, a classroom facility, and an infirmary. It was the source of an old Rutgers name for NJC women, "Coopies." According to the current Douglass dean and historian Mary Hartman, the location of the Douglass "sacred path," from College Hall to the streetcorner opposite the old site of Cooper, was probably determined by the fact that these two buildings were the original "sacred axis" of the college.

▲
A much-expanded Cooper Hall. Photo probably from the 1950s.

◄
The original Cooper House. Date of photo unknown.

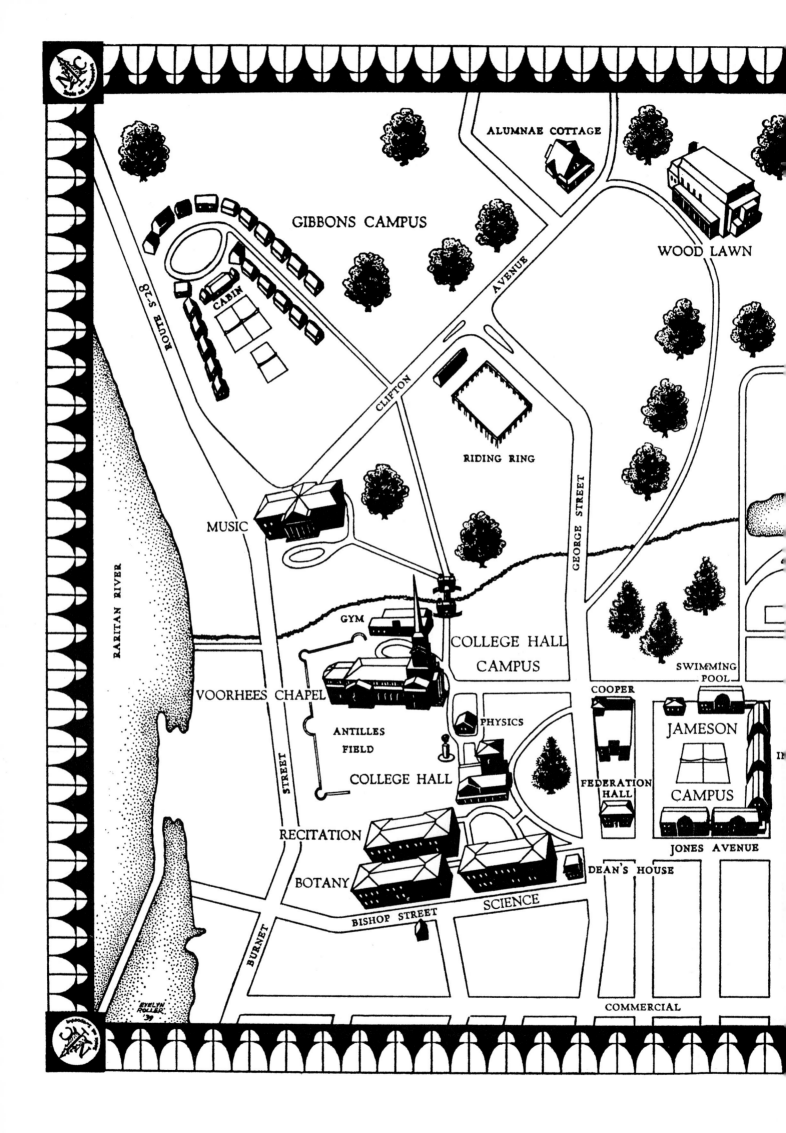

GIBBONS CAMPUS

ALUMNAE COTTAGE

WOOD LAWN

CABIN

RIDING RING

MUSIC

RARITAN RIVER

GYM

COLLEGE HALL
CAMPUS

SWIMMING
POOL

VOORHEES CHAPEL

COOPER

PHYSICS

JAMESON

ANTILLES
FIELD

FEDERATION
HALL

CAMPUS

COLLEGE HALL

RECITATION

JONES AVENUE

DEAN'S HOUSE

BOTANY

SCIENCE

BISHOP STREET

COMMERCIAL

EVELYN
ROLLER
'39

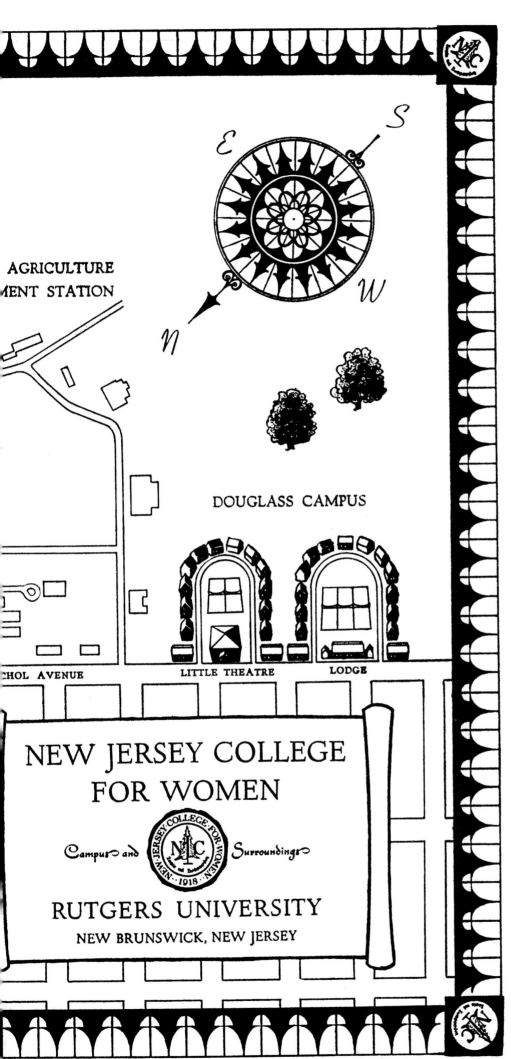

AGRICULTURE
MENT STATION

DOUGLASS CAMPUS

HOL AVENUE   LITTLE THEATRE   LODGE

NEW JERSEY COLLEGE FOR WOMEN

Campus and   *Surroundings*

RUTGERS UNIVERSITY

NEW BRUNSWICK, NEW JERSEY

▶
NJC, 1943
By NJC's twenty-fifth anniversary, the college had a decent physical plant, built mostly in the 1920s, thanks to Loree's financial management. The three major academic buildings—Recitation, Botany, and Science (whose names had no particular relation to the original uses)—were built off center, in a northern corner of the campus. This was done because Loree and Neilson feared that the plan for the new Route 1 would cut through the site of the buildings; the location was intended to bluff the highway department out of that route.

PASSION PUDDLE
The old farm pond at the College Farm, now called Passion Puddle, is the most photographed place at Cook College.

▶
The pond in the 1960s.

▼
The pond in 1901. The road used to go around the other side of the pond. The building is near the present site of Waller Hall.

South Jersey Club.

AGRICULTURAL SCHOOL

After World War I, the agricultural school continued to expand, both in its physical plant and its enrollment.

▶

Students at the College of Agriculture about 1920. The greenhouses are all still standing.

◀

The "country boys" from South Jersey studying agriculture, who became more numerous at Rutgers around the turn of the century, were sometimes the subject of satire, as this *Targum* sketch suggests.

▲
The new buildings at the Agricultural Experiment Station and the newly founded College of Agriculture in the 1920s. They are now named Thompson, Martin (Administration), and Bartlett halls. The school kept its practical agriculture close at hand; note the corn growing just across what is now Lipman Drive.

◀
Voorhees Library
The reading room in Voorhees Library, Rutgers'
second library after the Kirkpatrick gallery (or
its third, counting an original room at Old
Queen's). This photo is possibly from the
late 1920s.

◀
Panorama of Rutgers Students, 1920s
This panorama of the Old Queen's campus from
about 1920 is interestingly posed, with varying
clusters of students in formal and informal postures. About 220 figures appear in it, about half
the student body at the time. It was taken in the
early spring, but the occasion is not known. The
intention of a picture like this, and of the more
formal panorama of the cadets in Chapter 2
(pp. 92–93) was probably to show how big the
college had become. Today, it has the opposite
impact: Imagine a time when a good portion of
the college could have fit into one photo! Today,
if all the 44,000 students in the university lined
up in three rows, shoulder to shoulder, the re-
sulting picture would have to be almost three
miles wide. Rutgers College alone would be
about half a mile wide.

▼
WORLD WAR I
As elsewhere in the United States, sentiment at Rutgers became chauvinistic during World War I. In 1918 students—goaded on by a speech instructor—tarred and feathered a foreign-born student who refused to buy a war bond and paraded him down George Street. This postwar student humor suggests that by 1920 the Great War was already beginning to live in modern memory.

▲
HAZING, 1918
What the 1921 Rutgers student handbook referred to as a "little harmless hazing" was still practiced vigorously in the college after World War I. The handbook warned incoming students of sophomore attacks during the cane rush, the rope rush, the hat rush, the class banquet, the class picture, and chapel. It also described the "pyjamas peerade": "The Sophomores turn all the freshmen out in their pyjamas and march them down town in lock step. When the Juniors charge the column, the freshmen scatter and return to their rooms without being caught [they often were, or lost their pyjamas trying not to be]. The object being for the Sophomores to keep the Freshmen in line." In this 1918 yearbook cartoon of fearful freshmen hiding from sophomores, "Don't chip" refers to a prohibition on freshmen consorting with local women.

▶
CLASS CARICATURES
These class caricatures from 1920 are as vivid as those from 1886 (p. 57). The specifically collegiate dress has been elaborated further than it had been in the 1880s. These 1920 images show the influence of comic-strip drawing. Class caricatures disappear about the same time as the feelings of class unity wane, in the 1930s.

▼
FRESHMEN, 1915

A snapshot of three Rutgers freshmen in 1914, from the "memory book" of Roy F. Nichols '18. Although Nichols lived at home in his freshman year, he still managed to participate in most of the important events of undergraduate life. Nichols went on to become a Pulitzer Prize−winning historian and President of the American Historical Association. He was also a long-term trustee and a member of the Board of Governors at Rutgers.

▼
STUDENT LEXICON, 1920
By 1920 Rutgers was a less distinctive, insular world than the late-nineteenth-century college community. This Rutgers student lexicon from 1920 has forty words in it, less than half the number in the 1874 lexicon (p. 63). Only five words have survived from the earlier list: *bone, cram, cut, flunk,* and *rush.*

Life's Little Problem

ONE YEAR LATER - OF HIS OWN FREE WILL - BLOSSOM OUT WITH A HELMET LIKE THIS!

Ozzie Nelson '27

▲
BEANIES, 1920s
Freshmen were forced to wear unadorned beanies in the 1920s, the headwear later called the "dink." Sophomores and other classes happily wore their more elaborate class hats, with class numbers. From the *Chanticleer,* the short-lived Rutgers humor magazine of the mid-1920s (note the cartoonist's name).

Rutgers Campus Dictionary

ale, n.   Something not used at Faculty Smokers.

bluff, n.   Talk which does not mean all that it seems to.   v.   To perpetrate much talk.

bone, v.   To study hard.   n.   A person guilty of such foolishness.

bones, n.   Ivory cubes used in the pursuit of illicit amusement.

bull, n.   The imaginations of a fertile brain.   Commonly used in phrase "to shoot the bull."

butt, n.   Vulgar name for a cigarette.

cinch, n.   A course in which it is easy to bluff.   Vide, bluff.

crab, v.   The gentle art of destructive criticism.

crabber, n.   One addicted to the gentle art.

cram, v.   Attempting to do a year's work on the night before an examination.

crib, n.   A safeguard for Freshmen.   v.   To use such safeguards.

cut, n.   The result of oversleeping or lack of ambition.   v.   To stay away from a class.

debater, n.   A pugnacious fellow who is always chewing the rag.

desk, n.   Article of classroom furniture upon which everyone writes or carves his name.

dignity, n.   The President conducting chapel.

dining hall, n.   The main support of New Brunswick physicians.

dormitory, n.   A vile, ill-smelling place.

essay, n.   1,200 words from an old magazine.

fire insurance agent, n.   A preacher.

flunk, n.   A smiling acknowledgment of treacherous memory.   v.   To fail in a course or examination.

Freshman, n.   An unsaturated solution of sodium chloride.

grind, n.   One who came to college to study.

Holy Hill, n.   The residence of unbelievers in race suicide.

horse, n.   A handy little translation used by language students.

hot air, n.   A chemistry lecture.

instructor, n.   A water boy for a professor.

key, n.   A gold emblem given for proficiency in leg-pulling and bluffing.

laboratory, n.   A strange and wonderful place full of noxious odors.

lecture, n.   A sixty-minute nap; an interview with the President.

library, n.   One of the few places where the student can run bills.

manager, n.   A person who works the Athletic Association for his expenses.

over-cut, n.   Excess of absences, causing a student to repeat a course.

pony, n.   A small horse.   Vide, horse.

quiz, n.   Two hours' worth of questions to be answered in one.

rush, n.   Chronic differences of opinion between the under-classes.

slimer, n.   A name applied to Freshmen by Sophomores.

Sophomore, n.   A two-year-old Freshman.

stuck-out, n.   One who failed to use legitimate aids in examinations.

theolog, n.   A person who has his expenses paid by the Dutch Reformed Church.

trot, n.   A literal translation.   v.   To use such translations.

Class Warfare

By 1930 the college class had lost its hold on Rutgers students who gave their loyalties instead to the closer friendship groups found in dorm living units and especially in fraternities. The college was concerned; it saw a functional correlation among interclass warfare, class spirit, and college spirit—and college spirit was good for Rutgers. A report published in the *Rutgers Alumni Monthly*, analyzed similar happenings at other colleges. It concluded that the college had simply grown too large and diverse for the college class to remain a meaningful unit for the students, and it hoped that "college spirit" could be developed in other, less juvenile ways than by class warfare.

►

Class warfare was not quite dead, however, as these snapshots of an interclass snowball fight suggest (late 1920s).

►

◀
In the late 1930s the sophomores founded a group called the Keepers of the Queen's Traditions. The young man in the stocks is presumably a freshman who has failed to keep them.

▼
CLASS OF 1921
By the 1920s the Rutgers College class was not the little group of peers it had been in the late nineteenth century.

STUDENT RITUALS AT NJC

Nineteenth-century student rituals had been spontaneous developments. By the twentieth century, however, they had come to stand for college life and were carefully fostered by college authorities (many of whom had themselves been students in the late nineteenth century). The New Jersey College for Women, eager to establish its credentials, instituted student rituals immediately. The first graduating class, in 1922, observed Campus Night, the Christmas Dance, Mother's Day, Yule Log, and the "oldest custom: no student shall be seen off campus without a hat." Later, freshman costumes, Sacred Path, and Date with Dad were added.

◄
Members of the NJC Class of 1922 dancing around a Maypole on Mother's Day.

▼
The Yule Log Ceremony, held in College Hall prior to the completion of Voorhees Chapel in the late 1920s.

▼
College men and women, 1943. The men are probably from Rutgers. The women are definitely from NJC, Class of 1946, wearing the freshman costume designed for the war years: "a jaunty overseas cap with a long feather . . . a green Sam Browne belt with an enormous pouch containing freshman baggage, such as the Red Book, matches, and nickels. And a debonair touch is the little wooden sword . . . protection against the lordly . . . red-sweatered sophomores during the hazing period" (*Caellian*, 1943).

The "Inner Workings"
of the Faculty

▲
The faculty mind, an 1918 student view.

STUDENT HUMOR

Lacking the autonomous and relatively unsupervised publications of the late-nineteenth-century student, twentieth-century students were less exuberant in their satires of faculty, college, and community. But satire and subversion did occur. In 1936, for example, some sophomores and juniors, knowing President Clothier's sympathies in the forthcoming Roosevelt-Landon election, called Clothier, impersonating the Landon headquarters in New York. They told him that Landon would be honored to meet Clothier and any other sympathizers, and said that his campaign train would stop briefly in New Brunswick at three or four o'clock in the morning. Clothier and his aides trooped down to the station and were almost blown off the platform by the train, which was accelerating as it went through the station.

▼
A poem about the stereotypic professor, 1934.

THE PROFESSOR

Remote, serene the sage professor stands,
All ignorant of life's swift running sands.
His head is lost in clouds of dull the'ry,
His gaze benign is but deceptively cheery.
On guard against this wicked naughty world
His wooden sword is drawn, his flags unfurled;
He thinks his God-sent mission is reform—
Ah, he is far from his parental norm.
He's oft rebelliously quite beatific,
And, sometimes, harmlessly terrific.
His feet though sunk in life's infecting mud,
Placid he chews his intellectual cud.

CHANTICLEER

c., 1926   Price 25c

MOURNING NUMBER

HALL-MILLS CASE
Between 1922 and 1926, New Brunswick was nationally notorious for the Hall-Mills murder case. An Episcopalian minister and his choir-woman lover (residents of New Brunswick) were found murdered on a lovers' lane in Somerset in 1922. Eventually, suspicion fell on the minister's wife and brother-in-law, who lived in the house that presently is the residence of the dean of Douglass College. There was a widely reported trial in 1926, but no convictions. *Chanticleer* published a satire of the event that so upset the town fathers that they convinced the Rutgers president to suppress the magazine. Once again, the cartoonist was Ozzie Nelson. A later Rutgers alumni office eulogy of Nelson praised his humorous drawings, but the college could not have been happy with them at the time.

◀
Left: The original *Chanticleer* cover "Our Willie" is the ne'er-do-well brother-in-law, Willie Stevens, suspected of having hired the actual killers from the local New Brunswick underworld. Right: The expurgated cover.

SEXUALITY
The more open sexuality of the Roaring Twenties was apparent in Rutgers student publications.

◀
A montage of student wall decorations, Ford dormitory, 1923. The slogans are evidently from advertising and other parts of the popular press.

▶
QUEEN'S PLAYERS
These fine-looking gentlemen are in the Rutgers dramatic group, the Queen's Players, in the mid-1920s. The apparel must be a joke. Rutgers theatrical groups in the late nineteenth century had acted with faculty daughters and other local women. In the early twentieth century, young men sometimes played women's parts in college productions, but after the opening of the New Jersey College for Women in 1918, NJC students acted with the Queen's Players.

▼
From the *Chanticleer*, 1926.

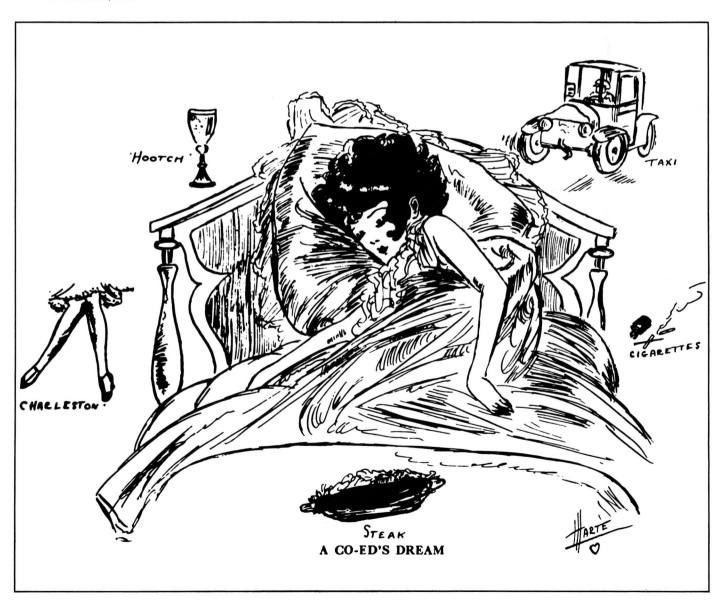

DeWinters '24

Pound

Social Life
With the availability of eligible young women at NJC, "social life" became salient at Rutgers for the first time in the 1920s.

▼
The Military Ball started in 1910 and was a favorite formal dance until the late 1960s. This photo, posed like a fashion-magazine spread, was taken in 1936. The trees were around Bishop House before the Bishop dorms were built in the 1950s.

A group of couples, 1936 yearbook; compare this photo to that of the fraternity houseparty from 1910 (p. 74). Here, men and women are grouped in pairs rather than in separate blocks. The chaperone is out of sight, though she was still required by university regulations at all fraternity parties in the 1930s—she could be hired from an approved list of respectable ladies supplied by the dean's office, or she might be one of the existing dormitory or fraternity housemothers (not all the fraternities were required to have them until 1945). At this time, unrelated young women were simply not allowed into student dorms at Rutgers College. Later, they were allowed into lounges on Sundays. For a while in the 1960s, they were allowed in rooms so long as the door was open as wide as a book. About the time the students refined that rule down to a "matchbook," the college dropped all such in loco parentis rules entirely.

A blissful young couple at a dance in 1939.

ADVERTISING
An advertising meditation on tobacco and wives, addressed to the college man in 1934.

FOOTBALL

Football continued to be the most important sport at Rutgers in the second, third, and fourth decades of the twentieth century. The yearbooks of the period always began their sports sections with football, which typically took as much space as all the other sports combined. Around World War I, the football rally became part of student life, initially as a spontaneous affair, later as an organized event to which freshmen were required to come. Homecoming, one of the few collegiate celebrations still observed at Rutgers, was invented in the 1930s.

Foster Sanford was Rutgers' first real professional coach, although he in fact donated his services. He had played on one of the great Yale football teams of the turn of the century and then had done some coaching. He built up a successful law practice in New York, but was continually being lured back to football. In 1913 Loree prevailed upon him to come to Rutgers and end its legendary losing streak in intercollegiate football. He produced a series of good teams until 1924; his era was the golden age of Rutgers football.

▶

The rules of twentieth-century football were still in flux, presenting unusual challenges to innovative coaches like Sanford. One of his inventions was the "hurdle play," in which a specialist from the track team was suited up in pants with leather loops and thrown over his own offensive line by two half-backs (he had used this play in pre-Rutgers days). Another was the "Rutgers formation," a human bulldozer in which two backs lined up, shoulders against buttocks, behind two offensive linesmen and power-assisted them in their initial charge. Both plays were eventually declared illegal by football authorities. But Sanford was a solid coach as well, who believed in "method, not men," and was widely hailed for producing outstanding teams with uneven talent. Ozzie Nelson remembered him as a "tough old man [who] . . . taught hard, rough football, specializing in the use of elbows and knees." He is a member of the National Football Hall of Fame.

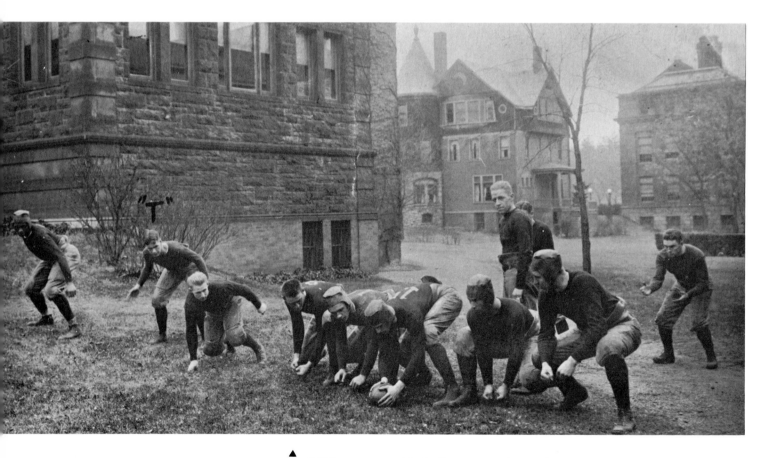

▲

The 1917 team was one of Sanford's greatest. In this posed action picture, not taken on the Rutgers campus, "T" is W. Herbert "Turk" Gardner, from whose album this photo was taken. The player on the far left is Paul Robeson, widely regarded as the best football player in the country that year and voted all-American at his position. Like most players of the day, Robeson played both offense and defense—offensive end and defensive fullback (the equivalent of modern middle linebacker). Rutgers lost only one game in 1917, to Syracuse (Princeton was not on the schedule that year).

ATHLETICS

ERIC FLEMING-'20

◀ A detail of football action, 1920 Rutgers yearbook and a modern-looking line charge compared to the scrumlike drawing from 1888 in chapter 2 (p. 76). Helmets, however, were apparently still optional.

▶ Professional coaches were well established at Rutgers by 1928. Second from the left, second row, is Harry J. Rockafeller, head coach. He had three assistant coaches, though they are not shown here (the other three men in coats and ties are student managers). The 1928 team went 6 and 3 for the season.

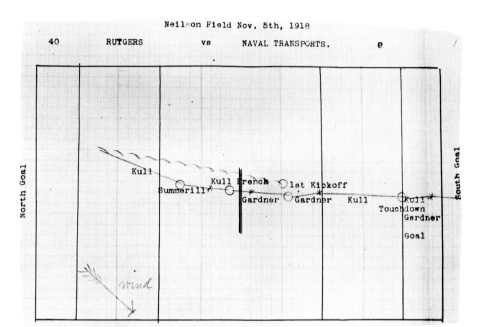

Neilson Field Nov. 5th, 1918
40   RUTGERS   vs   NAVAL TRANSPORTS.   0

◀ Rutgers' victory over Naval Transport in 1918, 40–0, was a particularly famous win; Naval Transport was a military-reserve team loaded with football talent from major schools. This is a set of plays from a playbook kept by "Turk" Gardner. Though the forward pass had been legalized in 1905, powerful running games still dominated college football and would continue to do so for years to come.

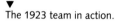

▼ The 1923 team in action.

▼
Neilson Field, the present site of the parking
deck and Records Hall. A photo of the Holy
Cross game in 1932, lost by Rutgers, 6–0.

◀
Carl R. Woodward, Jr., '40, as a natty young football fan at the Rutgers stadium, during his senior year.

▼
The 1938 football team inaugurated the new stadium by beating Princeton for the first time since 1869, by a score of 20–18. It was the most treasured Rutgers win in the twentieth century.

◀

LIVING ARRANGEMENTS

Students in Rutgers College dorms in the late 1970s believed that coed dorms were less ratty than all-men's dorms due to the greater natural cleanliness of women. With its almost monastic neatness, its minimal collegiate insignia, and its improvised lighting, this early-1920s female student's room (from Cooper Hall, NJC) supports all the same stereotypes. The dresser, incidentally, is the same model shown in the photo of the packing-crate gym (pp. 116–117), and alumnae from the 1940s through the 1970s remember the same furniture.

▼

A cozy scene in the recreation room of the Corwin Lodge, NJC, probably late 1920s.

▼
Rutgers College built its second dorm, Ford Hall, in 1915, and the Hegeman-Wessels-Quad complex in the late 1920s. These four students are outside Ford in the late 1920s; one may be selling hot dogs to the other three. Note the diversity of everyday college wear, starting a cut above the present norm (with the salesman) and increasing in formality from there.

The new dorms built in the late 1920s (Hegeman-Wessels-Quad) were made freshman dorms on the theory that class spirit would develop if the classes lived together. Housemothers and preceptors were also installed in them. This photo shows a freshman living group at Hegeman in 1937, displaying their nice diversity of footwear. The sophomore preceptor, John Isenmann '39, is sitting third from the left.

▼
These young men, probably in the late 1930s, were examples of the ability of off-campus students to cope with New Brunswick's traditionally crummy housing—a houseboat on the Raritan River.

FRATERNITIES

Fraternities were the heart of the extracurriculum at Rutgers between World War I and World War II. About half of the students lived in them, and fraternity men saw themselves as a social elite; "anyone who was anyone was in a fraternity," in the words of a Rutgers alumnus from the 1930s. Some had housemothers, others did not; until 1945 it was up to the individual chapter. Another alumnus believes that the hazing practiced routinely then would have shut any house down today (when hazing is literally against the law). The fraternities controlled campus politics through "combines" (voting alliances), and much of campus social life. A member of one of the top fraternities recalls that his house was serious about teaching its members social skills. Members had to be at dinner, in coat and tie, at a given hour. Attendance at the weekly meetings was strictly enforced—the meetings were held in fraternity regalia and run by strict parliamentary procedure. As in the 1860s and 1870s, however, antifraternity groups regularly emerged among nonfraternity upperclassmen—the Scarlet Barbarians in 1935, for example.

▼
Zeta Psi, 1939.

College Avenue Olympus

O, for to be a Zeta Psi
And sit on the front veranda looking every
    passerby
        in the eye;
And watching with a calm disdain
The unholy lowly as they walk by
On street terrain.
    Clad in the smartest soiled dungarees
    Give pedestrians well-executed freeze.
To recline in latest crimson jacket
Behind classic Greek colyumns,
Read "The Life of Henry VIII" by Hacket
And other learned volyumns.
    To feel oneself is the better

Of any other Greek letter.
    And not to give a fig
    For even a Kappa Sig.
    To single out with expert knowledge
    The one true type of J. Joe College,
    From the merely specious
    Or facetious.
In short—to live by regulation
In fraternal association.
In a kind of Rutgers Nirvana
A la Santayana.
For this, I wis,
Must be the highest bliss.

J. NAJAVITS

◄ A poem on the pleasures of fraternity snobbery, by a late-1930s Zeta Psi member. Published in the *Anthologist*, the student literary magazine founded in 1927.

▲ The fraternities of the 1930s and 1940s made no secret of one of their most fundamental hazing practices. A 1943 vignette.

THREE FAMOUS ALUMNI

Notable twentieth-century alumni of Rutgers include Clifford Case '25, U.S. senator from New Jersey; Sonny Werblin '31, developer of the New Jersey Meadowlands Sports Complex; Milton Friedman '32, economist; Martin Agronsky '36, news commentator; Frederick J. Kroesen '44, four-star general in World War II; and George Segal '63, sculptor. The three most famous, however—each typifying a different aspect of early-twentieth-century student life at Rutgers—are Selman Waksman, Paul Robeson, and Ozzie Nelson.

▶

Selman Waksman '15, exemplified the new eastern European immigrant populations entering the United States in the late nineteenth and early twentieth century. Like Jacob Lipman, his mentor at Rutgers, Waksman was a Russian-born Jew. Waksman wanted to become a doctor, but Lipman encouraged him to study soil science at Rutgers. As an undergraduate Waksman was president of the Menorah Society, the first Jewish organization at Rutgers. This photo is from his gymnasium graduation in Russia, 1910.

▼
GRANDFATHER'S CLUB

From the early twentieth century, Rutgers began to take pride in its lineages, in families who had sent generation after generation to the school. These youths from the 1930s, sons and grandsons of alumni, are another example of the elaboration of collegiate dress at the time: one young man is in an everyday outfit of coat and tie, the other three are each dressed for a different sport.

TIME

THE WEEKLY NEWSMAGAZINE

MICROBIOLOGIST WAKSMAN
"The remedies are in our own backyards."

Waksman did graduate work at the University of California and returned to Rutgers as a professor of microbiology. In the course of research on soil microorganisms, he discovered streptomycin, the cure for tuberculosis. He coined the word *anti-biotic* and founded the Institute of Microbiology. In 1952 he received the Nobel Prize. And in 1949, he achieved the ultimate personal accolade in American society—a *Time* magazine cover.

Paul Robeson '19, was the third black student at Rutgers, born the son of a black clergyman in Princeton and educated in Somerville. Robeson was an all-American football player at Rutgers, won letters in most of the other sports, was a debating champion, and was elected to Phi Beta Kappa. He was hazed unmercifully by the football team as a first-year player, and he may not have been made welcome in the Glee Club. But generally, Rutgers was very proud of him in his student days and seems to have treated him reasonably well. He is shown here as a member of the Varsity Club of 1917–1918.

Robeson went on to a distinguished career as an actor, singer (he had a magnificent operatic voice), and political activist. In the 1950s he was controversial for his internationalism and declared admiration for the Soviet Union. Since the 1960s his stature has again been recognized (except by the National Football Hall of Fame, which inexplicably has still not inducted him). He is shown here acting in a Hollywood production of *The Emperor Jones* in the early 1930s.

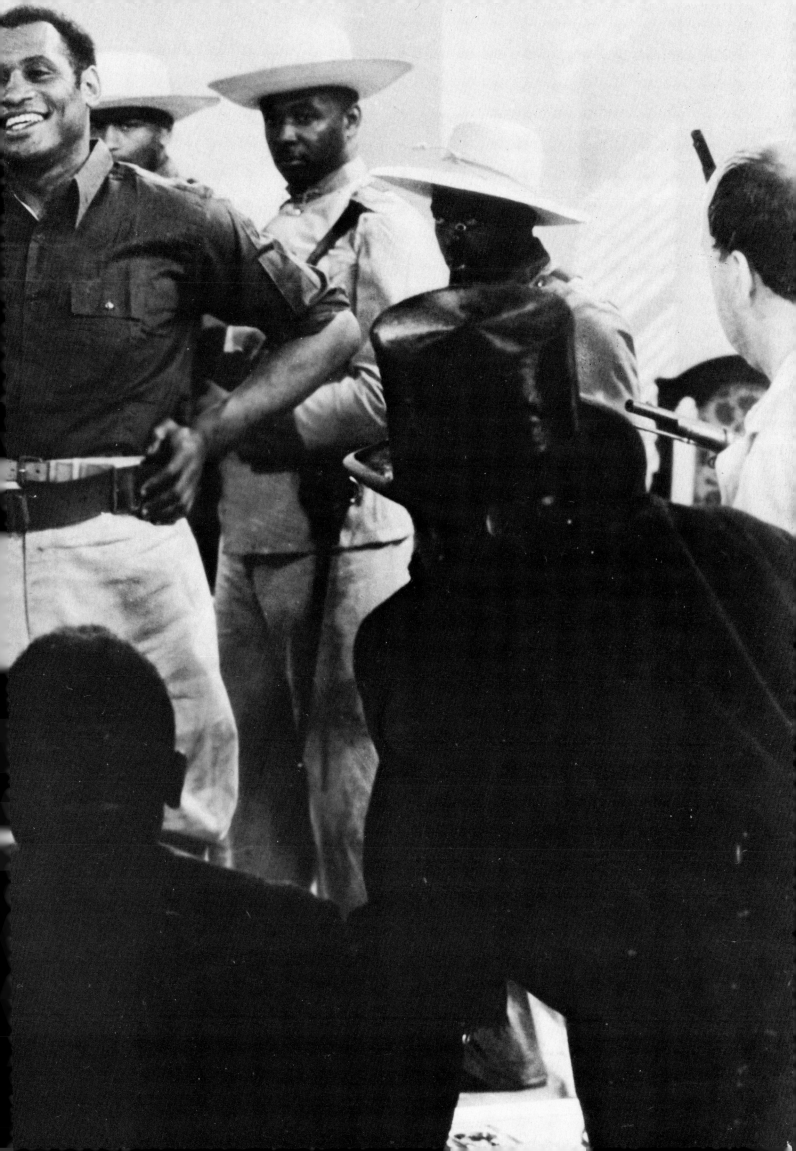

▼
Ozzie Nelson '27, was a golden boy all the way. At Rutgers, Nelson, born in Jersey City, was on the football team, edited and drew cartoons for the humor magazine, acted, directed the band, and debated. He says that he had plenty of time for extracurricular activities since he took the "fresh air" course (modern students would call it a "gut major")—a combination of political science and English. The photo shows him with three other apparent Big Men on Campus (Nelson is on the far left) in front of Old Queen's sometime in the mid-1920s.

▶
After college, Nelson led a popular big band (and made the football song "Loyal Sons of Rutgers" famous), married his singer, and went on to a career on radio and TV. In the 1950s and 1960s, the "Ozzie and Harriet Show" presented the all-American family in weekly episodes. Until his death in 1975, Nelson was himself a loyal son of Rutgers. Here he is receiving an award from a Rutgers alumni club in California in 1961.

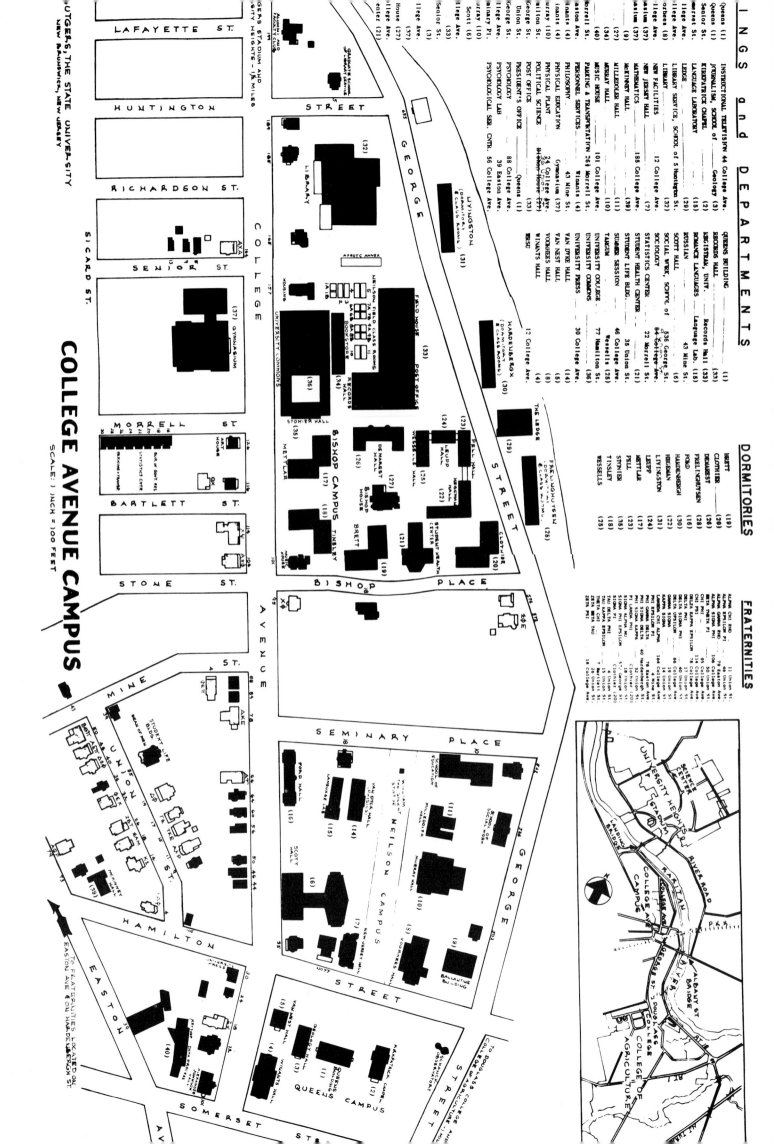

COLLEGE AVENUE CAMPUS

SCALE: 1 INCH = 100 FEET

RUTGERS, THE STATE UNIVERSITY
NEW BRUNSWICK, NEW JERSEY

BUILDINGS and DEPARTMENTS

Queens (1)	QUEENS BUILDING	(1)
Queens (1)	RECORDS HALL	(33)
Senior St.	REGISTRAR, UNIV.	Records Hall (33)
Morrell St.	ROMANCE LANGUAGES	Language Lab. (18)
College Ave.	RUSSIAN	43 Mine St.
Ledge	SCOTT HALL	(6)
Library Service, School of 5 Huntington St.	SOCIAL WORK, SCHOOL of	536 George St.
College Ave. (8)	LIBRARY	12 College Ave. (32)
College Ave. (8)	SOCIOLOGY	84 College Ave.
College Ave. (37)	NEW JERSEY HALL	(7)
Geology (3)	STATISTICS CENTER	22 Morrell St.
McKinney Hall (9)	MATHEMATICS	185 College Ave.
McKinney Hall (9)	STUDENT HEALTH CENTER	(21)
McKinney Hall (39)	STUDENT LIFE BLDG.	35 Union St.
Jameson (27)	SUMMER SESSION	46 College Ave.
(27)	TARGUM	Wessells (26)
(34)	UNIVERSITY COLLEGE	77 Hamilton St.
(40)	UNIVERSITY COMMONS	(36)
Morrell St.	UNIVERSITY PRESS	30 College Ave.
Easton Ave.	VAN DYKE HALL	(14)
(4)	VAN NEST HALL	(5)
(4)	VOORHEES HALL	(8)
Murray (4)	WINANTS HALL	(4)
(10)	NBSU	
George St.	POST OFFICE	
Union (1)	PRESIDENT'S OFFICE	Queens (1)
George St.	PSYCHOLOGY	88 College Ave.
(27)	PSYCHOLOGY	39 Easton Ave.
(37)	PSYCHOLOGICAL SER. CNTR.	56 College Ave.

INSTRUCTIONAL TELEVISION 44 College Ave.
JOURNALISM, SCHOOL of
KIRKPATRICK CHAPEL (2)
LANGUAGE LABORATORY (18)
LIBRARY SERVICE, SCHOOL of 5 Huntington St. (29)
NEW FACILITIES
MILLEDOLER HALL (10)
MURRAY HALL (10)
MUSIC HOUSE
PARKING & TRANSPORTATION 261 Morrell St.
PERSONNEL SERVICES
PHILOSOPHY 43 Mine St.
PHYSICAL EDUCATION Gymnasium (37)
PHYSICAL PLANT 26 College Ave.
POLITICAL SCIENCE Bishop House (17)
(33)

DORMITORIES

BRETT	(19)
CLOTHIER	(20)
DEMAREST	(26)
FRELINGHUYSEN	(28)
FORD	(16)
HARDENBERGH	(22)
HEGEMAN	(22)
LEUPP	(24)
LIVINGSTON	(31)
METTLAR	(17)
PELL	(23)
STONIER	(35)
TINSLEY	(18)
WESSELLS	(25)

FRATERNITIES

ALPHA CHI RHO	11 Union St.
ALPHA EPSILON PI	46 Union St.
ALPHA GAMMA RHO	79 Easton Ave.
ALPHA SIGMA PHI	106 College Ave.
BETA THETA PI	30 Union St.
CHI PHI	114 College Ave.
CHI PSI	78 College Ave.
DELTA KAPPA EPSILON	17 Union St.
DELTA PHI	66 College Ave.
DELTA SIGMA PHI	40 Union St.
DELTA UPSILON	19 Union St.
GAMMA SIGMA	14 Union St.
KAPPA SIGMA	18 College Ave.
LAMBDA CHI ALPHA	164 College Ave.
PHI EPSILON PI	78 Easton Ave.
PHI GAMMA DELTA	40 Hardenbergh St.
PHI SIGMA KAPPA	32 Union St.
PI LAMBDA PHI	18 Union St.
SIGMA ALPHA MU	3 George St.
SIGMA PHI EPSILON	Clothier (20)
TAU DELTA PHI	4 Union St.
TAU EPSILON PHI	Bartlett St.
TAU KAPPA EPSILON	19 Union St.
THETA CHI	26 Union St.
ZETA BETA TAU	18 College Ave.
ZETA PSI	

TO FRATERNITIES LOCATED ON
EASTON AVE & ON HARDENBERGH ST

TO COLLEGE of AGRICULTURE and
DOUGLASS COLLEGE

"RU" 1945–The Present

Rutgers history before World War II is an uncertain business, with only occasional evidence that its leaders had a clear vision of what the college and university ought to be, and how it ought to go about achieving its goals. This changed after the war. In different ways, the three principal postwar presidents—Lewis Webster Jones, Mason Gross, and Edward Bloustein—all understood and acted consistently on the implications of the New Jersey legislature's formal designation of Rutgers as the State University of New Jersey in 1945: to the degree that Rutgers could manage its relations with the State of New Jersey, it could grow into a firmly rooted, major institution of higher education.

If state-supported growth has indeed been the goal of Rutgers leadership since the war, then Rutgers has been an impressive success. In 1948 the university (the men's colleges, NJC, the newly attached University of Newark, University College, and the then-small graduate school) had been swollen by the returning veterans to what looked at the time like a vast horde of students—a total of 8,656. After a lull in the early 1950s, however, this enrollment turned out to be only a warm-up. With the help of state bonds between 1959 and the early 1970s, Rutgers engaged in the massive expansion of its physical plant in New Brunswick, Newark, and Camden, constructing or renovating about eighty buildings during Mason Gross's tenure alone (1959–1970). Since the mid-1970s, the entire university has typically had over 40,000 students in a given year—44,854 were the figures in 1984, including 26,737 undergraduates, taught by 2,500 faculty members, managed by 1,071 administrative and professional personnel, and supported by 1,462 secretaries.

From the student point of view, however, there have been some losses. On the one hand, postwar Rutgers students have often been relatively serious-minded youths in search of a useful and economical college education. With ninety-four areas of study available to undergraduates at the New Brunswick campuses, taught by a competent, nationally ranked faculty—and with tuition rates at the upper range of those of state universities but still well below most private colleges—Rutgers has usually provided what they wanted. On the other hand, the decline of a sense of student community noticeable at Rutgers in the early twentieth century has if anything accelerated since the war. One measure of this loss may be detected in student vocabularies. Students at Rutgers, like students in other colleges, take pleasure in their slang and have published slang lexicons every ten or twenty years since the 1870s. The lexicons are a handy index of the degree to which the college is a speech community, a tightly knit world of common understandings, felt to be distinctively different from the world outside. A Rutgers student lexicon from 1874 contains 84 different terms (see p. 63); a lexicon from 1920 contains 40 (see p. 131); and a recent one from 1980 contains only 13 (see p. 222). And some of these 1980 terms have already disappeared, replaced by high-school slang.

There is nothing surprising about the loss of a feeling of community at Rutgers in the twentieth century. It is consistent with general trends in modern American society, where, with some justification, every generation has looked back nostal-

◄

College Avenue Map, 1960
Map of the College Avenue Campus about 1960, before the construction of the student center.

gically on the life of the last as smaller in scale, more localized, and more personal—
at the small town or at the old urban neighborhood as well as at the small college.
Rutgers' changes have been more extreme, however, for Rutgers has grown more
rapidly and altered its self-image more radically than almost any other American
college or university. Student community is also a particularly poignant subject at
Rutgers because of the university's efforts since the 1960s to keep college spirit alive
in a large university—with the Livingston and Cook College experiments.

Student life began to change quickly during World War II, when enrollment
fluctuated wildly, most of campus life shut down, and a good deal of educational
activity was devoted to the Army Specialized Training Program (ASTP). After the
war, the veterans arrived, funded by the GI Bill. Enrollment in the men's colleges
increased from 750 in 1945 to 4,200 in 1948, with many of the students housed
and educated in temporary structures put up during the war. On the one hand, as
Richard P. McCormick notes, the veterans seemed eager to reconstruct conventional campus life as quickly as possible, reestablishing the newspaper, the campus
organizations, and traditional social activities. On the other hand, when things did
not go well, the veterans were more likely to be vocal than Rutgers students usually
had been in the past, criticizing administrative inertia strongly in the late 1940s and
launching another attack on the fraternities, this time on their discrimination. Initially, the college did not cope very well with its postwar expansion. Conditions to
which the modern student is more accustomed were first being felt in college: in
McCormick's words, "long lines at registration, at the bookstore, and in the Commons; overcrowded classrooms; a frustrating shortage of parking spaces; time-
consuming [commuting]." In a later reminiscence, a retired dean of men, Cornelius
Boocock, remembered the late 1940s as a time when "the students thought that no
one cared about them and that Rutgers was a hell of a place."

By the 1950s, however, the college had quieted down. Student services had
improved, the veterans had graduated, conventional adolescents again began to
dominate incoming classes, and enrollment declined. The whole decade was relatively placid at Rutgers, just as it was at other American colleges; in 1959, in fact,
CBS Television made Rutgers undergraduates exemplars of all American college
youth in a two-hour special that was shot at the college and broadcast under the
title "Generation without a Cause." Social life continued to center on the fraternities, which still enrolled about half the student body. One popular campus event
for a few years—a revival of a late-nineteenth-century outing—was a boat trip up
the Hudson. But no one got very excited about any "traditional" collegiate activities, for like students today, students in the 1950s thought of themselves as individ-
ualists not willing to let their behavior be defined by any group, though a subtler
general conformism was pervasive.

Sports also generated much less excitement than at any time in the previous
history of the college since the 1870s. The teams in the 1950s were not very il-
lustrious, though prior generations of Rutgers students had not let athletic failure

dampen their enthusiasm. During a brief period of success in 1959, a Rutgers all-American football player told the national press that "at Rutgers, football is a part of college, not college a part of football"—an attitude in which the university took some pride. Rutgers remained officially opposed to big-time sports through Mason Gross's presidency, so much so that when an alumnus surprisingly gave the school $3 million in 1966 to "beef up football," the administration said that the money would be useful for sports scholarships, but pledged that it would have no effect on sports policy.

The 1950s were not entirely uneventful, however, and the students were not entirely apolitical. In the early 1950s they joined the faculty in condemning the administration's unwillingness to stand behind two faculty members smeared by the McCarthy investigations; and in 1958 they became angry enough about state underfunding of Rutgers to send 700 demonstrators to Trenton. In the latter case, student concerns coincided closely with administrative concerns; a second, much larger wave of enrollment was about to sweep over higher education, the product of the postwar baby boom, and New Jersey had thumpingly voted down the first state bond issue proposed to fund New Jersey colleges in 1948. President Jones dealt with one of the state's grievances in 1956 by supporting the creation of a state-dominated Board of Governors, which succeeded the older Board of Trustees of the privately controlled university. And in 1957 the Sputnik crisis linked higher education and Cold War patriotism in the minds of most Americans, and higher education suddenly became publicly fundable, even in the state of New Jersey. In 1959, 1964, and 1968 New Jersey voters approved multimillion-dollar bond issues; together with newly available federal funds, these provided Rutgers with more than $200 million for capital development in the next decade, and—under President Gross—expansion began in earnest.

Through the 1950s and 1960s new dorms, classrooms, libraries, and research buildings went up at what was now called the College Avenue Campus (the old Rutgers College Campus), at University Heights, at Douglass (as the New Jersey College for Women had renamed itself in 1955), at Newark (added to Rutgers in 1946) and at Camden (added in 1950). In the mid-1960s the first of what in those heady days were to be three new colleges on the Kilmer tract in Piscataway was inaugurated—Livingston. In the financially retracting early 1970s (when one more bond issue was approved), the second of these colleges became Cook College, located across town because that was where the faculty needed for an "ecological" college was already located—and the third college was quietly canceled. About this time, Rutgers College was recreated as an entity and given its own dean, after almost half a century during which it had been administratively labeled the various men's colleges. When Edward J. Bloustein succeeded Mason Gross in 1971, he inherited six campuses, soon to be seven, not to mention a University College spread over three campuses, a rapidly expanding graduate school, and a number of autonomous research centers. He also inherited the late 1960s, the most interesting and traumatic period in the history of American college youth since the late nineteenth century.

The trajectory of student politics at Rutgers in the 1960s was like that of American college students elsewhere: Kennedy-era activism followed by a more radical confrontational style. Starting in the late 1950s, Rutgers student publications began to show an intense interest in national affairs unprecedented at Rutgers since the days of the early-nineteenth-century student literary societies. In the early 1960s, Peace Corps activities and the National Student Association were particularly prestigious on campus, and there was also conservative activity among the students linked to the Goldwater movement. Student critics once again attacked the fraternities and the few remnants of college class rituals. To "discriminate" against freshmen by making them wear "dinks," according to a 1961 *Targum* editorial, was like discriminating against blacks in the South. The office of the dean of men declared the "dink" henceforth voluntary (it disappeared entirely about 1970), and canceled the interclass tourney between the sophomores and the freshmen—the last trace of class warfare first invented by Rutgers students in the mid-1860s and later supported by the early-twentieth-century Rutgers deans.

The mood of the students changed in the mid-1960s, as the Vietnam War became more unpopular and the students became increasingly vulnerable to the draft. The first big student demonstrations occurred in 1965, when the distinguished Rutgers historian Eugene Genovese spoke out against the Vietnam War and a candidate for governor of New Jersey called for his dismissal (President Gross supported Genovese). Demonstrations accelerated in 1967; they were "bound to happen at Rutgers, too," the *Rutgers Alumni Magazine* announced with a sigh at the end of that year. The magazine proceeded glumly to chronicle a confrontational era that lasted about five years—mostly demonstrations in favor of minority education, and against the war and on-campus ROTC. The university responded by reinforcing Livingston College's minority mission, by instituting black studies and the EOF program, by attempting to increase minority faculty appointments, and by redefining ROTC as an elective. By 1972 ROTC had only 196 student cadets, 10 percent of the number five years earlier.

At Rutgers as elsewhere, a social and cultural revolution was occurring. Since the Civil War, each generation of college students had marked itself off as an elite within American youth, wearing different clothes and speaking a different language from noncollegiate youths. Now students sought to develop a nationwide, classless youth movement. Etiquette and dress changed radically, from the distinctive college clothing in fashion up to the early 1960s, to blue jeans, T-shirts, army jackets and long hair loosely modeled on older working-class fashions. Favorite musical groups as late as the early 1960s had been college-oriented, like the Kingston Trio or Peter, Paul and Mary; now they were heavy rock bands ultimately inspired by black music. Sexual norms changed so rapidly that when Rutgers College became coeducational in 1972 and immediately installed coed dorms, there was no criticism to speak of in the state.

Many of these developments, however, made college elders very unhappy. The alumni magazine noted with alarm the growing drug use on campus, and in May 1970 a historian from the Class of 1927 compared the adolescent youth culture of the 1920s to the political youth culture of the 1960s, making his preferences clear: "Aren't you glad we were young when we were young? We cut up, but not with knives, bottles and Molotov cocktails. We had our generation gap . . . it's the way kids start making a world of their own. We made a nice one which is fun to remember." Legislators and other citizens complained that the university was not being tough enough with student demonstrators. Campus patrol was rapidly expanded and eventually renamed the Rutgers University Police. The official justification for its expansion was the growing crime rate on the increasingly open and vulnerable campuses; but an obvious additional function of a larger police force was to give the university the means to suppress student disorders.

Many faculty members, students, and administrators at Rutgers during the late 1960s remember President Gross with remarkable affection, and credit his accessibility and willingness to talk with anyone with keeping events from becoming even more explosive than they were. President Bloustein had a less-personal, less-gregarious style and was stricter with student disruption, but he also took significant activist positions of his own. In 1972 he lead an antiwar delegation to Washington; he increased the university's commitment to more-equitable employment and education of women; and he helped keep minority education alive in the less-favorable climate of the late 1970s and early 1980s.

At Rutgers, 1970 or so was the nadir of the traditional student way of life inherited from the late nineteenth century. In 1965 student pressure led to the appointment of a joint committee that initiated the end of in loco parentis, effectively declaring that the college was no longer concerned with the private behavior of its students—with their morality. In 1967, housemothers were taken out of the fraternities; they had been officially placed there in 1945 to improve the "moral tone" of the houses. Fraternities were already on the downswing. By 1970 they enrolled only a quarter of the campus population and were seriously worried about their survival. Judging from their yearbook photos, fraternity members joined other students about this time in abandoning the formal clothing that had hitherto marked the "college man." Freshman dorms were abandoned in the early 1960s, on the grounds that interclass dorms were neater and less rowdy; but the action also recognized the fact that college class solidarity now had almost no significance to anyone—student or dean. Football had even less hold on student enthusiasm than in the 1950s; the traditional pep rally before the Rutgers-Princeton game was discontinued in 1971.

Livingston College, first opened for students in 1969, was the university's most serious attempt to keep a sense of student community alive in the era of the large university. Though Livingston was to be small, it was not intended to be old-fashioned. Its mission was social relevance; it recruited nationally an impressive, committed faculty; and it looked for minority students and "unconventional" nonminority students. The internal organization of Livingston mirrored its aims, especially in its attempt to minimize authority relations between faculty and students. Grading was de-emphasized, a controversial faculty-student bicameral legislature was installed, and it was planned that the faculty members would share eating facilities with the students, and some would share housing with them, in "residences" rather than in "dorms."

Both faculty members and students remember the first few years at Livingston as a time of creativity and excitement, and many early alumni express gratitude to the college for being the sort of place that was willing to give them a chance at a college education when other schools were unwilling or unsuitable. But as an experiment in college organization, Livingston as originally conceived was soon in trouble. Internal racial tensions dimmed some of the initial idealism; the original campus was isolated from the rest of the university and from the urban world to which it was intended to be relevant; and it lacked many amenities to brighten up on-campus life. Nor did the militancy of many of the students help its image in the wider university or in the state. An evaluation in 1971 praised its innovative pedagogy but attacked its "ineffective administration"—its "almost mystic notion" that because Livingston was unique, "no structures were needed." A new dean took over and established more conventional procedures.

When President Bloustein came into office, he found a vast, diverse, administratively and geographically decentralized institution that had grown too quickly for its own good. Each college had competing deans and faculty, and the conduct of coherent, universitywide academic departments and graduate programs was particularly difficult. Such basic things as the number of students enrolled in the whole university were not known by the central administration. At the same time, the state of New Jersey—in the form of the Board of Higher Education (created in 1966)—was becoming increasingly aggressive in its demands for accountability. Bloustein defended university autonomy in many areas and responded to other managerial questions when he felt they were legitimate ones; he is generally credited with bringing about the best relations with the state of New Jersey in the history of the university. He revamped the administration and continues to do so, pursuing centralization and bureaucratic rationalization—the Federated System in the 1970s (proposed in the 1960s, well before he arrived) and the more systematic Reorganization since 1980. Not everything has been centralized, however; there is an attempt at present to maintain localized student life in the colleges by keeping college deanships intact and by somewhat decentralizing student services.

The small undergraduate college has not disappeared at Rutgers in the mid-1980s. Livingston, Cook, and Douglass each have an undergraduate enrollment in the range of 3,000. Rutgers College is considerably larger, climbing to around 8,000 undergraduates after the advent of coeducation. Research in several Rutgers College dormitories in the late 1970s indicated a relatively unstructured student culture based more on the values of general late-adolescent American youth culture in the

1970s than on anything particularly collegiate, let alone specifically "Rutgersian." The most focused image of Rutgers was a negative image of its bureaucracy—the so-called "Rutgers Screw." The new dress code from the late 1960s was still in effect. Rutgers men generally wore blue jeans, T-shirts, and sneakers; Rutgers women wore better-tailored versions of the same, and more formally dressed women tended to be labeled "Debbie Douglasses." Musical preference often signaled racial or gender identity; stereotypically, rock for whites and disco for blacks, louder for men and mellower for women. These preferences, however, were not linked in any discernible way to being in college—they were the tastes typical of Americans in their late teens and early twenties. The old Rutgers songs were curiosities known only to the specialists in the choral groups or to those fraternity members whose initiation required their memorizing these songs. College sports aroused little enthusiasm. The pranks and other juvenile fun of the earlier collegiate way of life continued to thrive among freshmen and sophomores in the dorms and fraternities (with water fights, minor vandalism, informal hazing of unpopular peers, and mock kidnappings), but students in the late 1970s generally took college seriously and expected their education to contribute to professional success later in life. They studied an average of three or four hours a day during the week, undoubtedly more than the Rutgers average in the nineteenth or early twentieth century. They respected the faculty members as specialists who "know their stuff" (but often "don't know how to teach it"), but they rarely knew any faculty members personally, and they hardly ever imagined going into academia themselves. Obvious intellectuals seemed rare among the students, both because there were not many of them and because those who were around had learned to keep quiet about their interests.

Relations between men and women in the coed dorms were orderly and generally discreet, with many group-enforced norms of behavior. Interracial relations were tenser, but were often handled with considerable sensitivity by all concerned. Students gave most of their extracurricular attention to their networks of friends (spending about three hours a day in informal activities with friends), whom they most typically met in the dorms and fraternities, and occasionally in classes and in activity groups. They gave less time to formal campus organizations or activities, and probably more students practiced sports informally (running, weight lifting, and intramurals) than devoted themselves to watching Rutgers teams. Fraternity life continued at a low level, with about 25 percent of the male undergraduates as members. Fraternity membership no longer served to mark distinctions in social status among the students, as it had in the 1950s and earlier; students joined fraternities for the sake of a sense of brotherhood in an impersonal university, for housing, and for the parties. Thursday night was traditionally party night; like many of the faculty members, the students tried to avoid Friday classes and often left town for three-day weekends.

Similar research at Rutgers College in 1984 suggests changes in student life since the late 1970s, some of them changes back toward the traditions. Though the basic, informal dress of Rutgers students remains jeans, T-shirts, and running shoes, a preppie, or collegiate, look is increasingly popular, often among student leaders in particular. *Preppie* does not refer to the jackets and ties of the earlier college look, however; typically, it is an alligator shirt, pleated pants, and loafers. The style of preppie clothes for women is derived from those of the men—perhaps a vestige of Rutgers' identity as a men's school. Many students enjoy the new emphasis—emanating from the office of the dean of students—on Rutgers tradition and history. More Rutgers insignia and other signs of university spirit are visible in dorm rooms, and the rejuvenated football team is generating student interest, at least so long as it continues to win. Fraternity membership is about what it was in the late 1970s, but the new sororities are increasingly popular among the women, with six chapters and about one-fifth of the women undergraduates of Rutgers College as members. The college honors program and higher standards of freshman recruiting have resulted in a sprinkling of students in the dorms who have interests more manifestly intellectual than was apparent in the late 1970s.

At the same time, in such things as their increasingly elaborate party clothes—the "*GQ* look" for men—and in their tastes in music, students in the 1980s remain members of a youth culture to which collegiate identity is irrelevant. Rutgers students speak of college as a place of choice rather than conformity, and they see Rutgers as an especially diverse institution, often in contrast to Princeton. Behavioral conformity continues to be as important as it is elsewhere in American society although actual tolerance of nontraditional student life styles seems reasonably well established within Rutgers student culture.

Although modern Rutgers students do not devote their off-hours to intense literary activities, in other ways—oddly enough—they have come back full circle to the characteristics of college life at Rutgers in the early nineteenth century. With the breakdown of in loco parentis, modern students have almost as much personal autonomy as the early-nineteenth-century students living in boardinghouses downtown. They would probably agree with early-nineteenth-century students that there are unique "pleasures of student life," but that these do not necessarily entail any particular commitment to Rutgers as an institution or to many of the late-nineteenth-century practices—intercollegiate sports, college songs, hazing and rushing, and the rest. Like early-nineteenth-century students, they generally find the intensely juvenile activities of the late-nineteenth and early-twentieth-century student beneath them—"high-school stuff," in twentieth-century parlance. Like early-nineteenth-century students, they get very involved in political and social issues, periodically at least. At the same time, like most modern Americans, they are often alienated from rich personal relationships by the bureaucratic settings in which they live and by their own individualistic values. At times they yearn for a sense of community, and late-nineteenth-century collegiate forms were the epitome of college community. If students in the 1980s are indeed returning to traditions, the late nineteenth century is their most obvious source of precedents—one current example is the recent revival of the senior honor society, Cap and Skull.

Over the last 150 years, the creativity of Rutgers students, like that of other American college students, has been impressive. In the early nineteenth century, they anticipated the curriculum reforms of the late nineteenth century. In the late nineteenth century, they invented a way of life that became perhaps the principal attraction to college for early-twentieth-century American youth. And in the late 1960s they pushed the university into fundamental changes in its treatment of minorities—and of students in general—which are still with us today. Rutgers students continue to pose a challenge and offer an opportunity to the modern university. If this brief history has any lesson at all, it's that there's no telling what they'll come up with next.

SCENES

At least two hundred million dollars were spent on university construction between the late 1950s and the early 1970s, completely transforming the physical environment within which the students lived. The post–World War II architecture of Rutgers is generally neither better nor worse than that of most other rapidly expanding universities. There are occasional felicities: the Douglass library and art complex, for example, which fit beautifully into the natural setting of the ravine. But on the whole, the modern architecture of Rutgers does not compare to that of the architecturally cohesive universities— Princeton or Cornell, for instance. Given the sprawl of the university, it is also difficult to photograph the architecture well. Aerial photographs give the best sense of the scale of contemporary Rutgers, and the many images of demolition and construction give a sense of how radically Rutgers changed in appearance after World War II.

▼
NJC CAMPUS, LATE 1940s
An aerial photo of the NJC campus just after the war, before the construction of the student center at the corner of Nichol and George. The packing-crate gym is the first building to the right of the chapel.

◄
COLLEGE AVENUE CAMPUS, LATE 1940s
An aerial view of the College Avenue Campus just after the war. Records Hall, the large building in the central foreground covered most of the old Neilson football field. Records Hall was intended to be an aircraft building in Russia, but when the war ended, it was redirected to Rutgers from its depot in Hillsborough. For years, it served as the student commons. Behind it, along the river, are emergency classrooms built during the war; the "river dorms" are now in their place. The Bishop dorms (Mettlar, etc.) are not yet built, and parking does not yet appear to be a problem.

▼
THE LIBRARY
"The Librarian's Dilemma": University Librarian Donald Cameron looks over a week's supply of bound periodicals, inadequately stored in the overcrowded Voorhees Library. Photo probably taken in the mid-1950s.

▼
The foundations of Alexander Library, mid-1950s, built on a site formerly occupied by the Prep School dormitory houses, just northwest of the Neilson Field. This photo was taken not far from the spot shown in the 1890s picture of the first clearing of the football field (p. 78).

THE LEDGE

Rutgers made its first major investment in facilities for the one-quarter to one-third of its students who commute with the construction of the Ledge in 1957. The name is not a random choice. There had been a sharp drop along this side of the campus for years; one of Paul Robeson's classmates recalled falling down it into the canal one afternoon while fooling around on the way back from Neilson Field and being heroically pulled out by Robeson.

▼
One of the first uses of the Ledge was as an emergency infirmary during the flu epidemic of the fall of 1957.

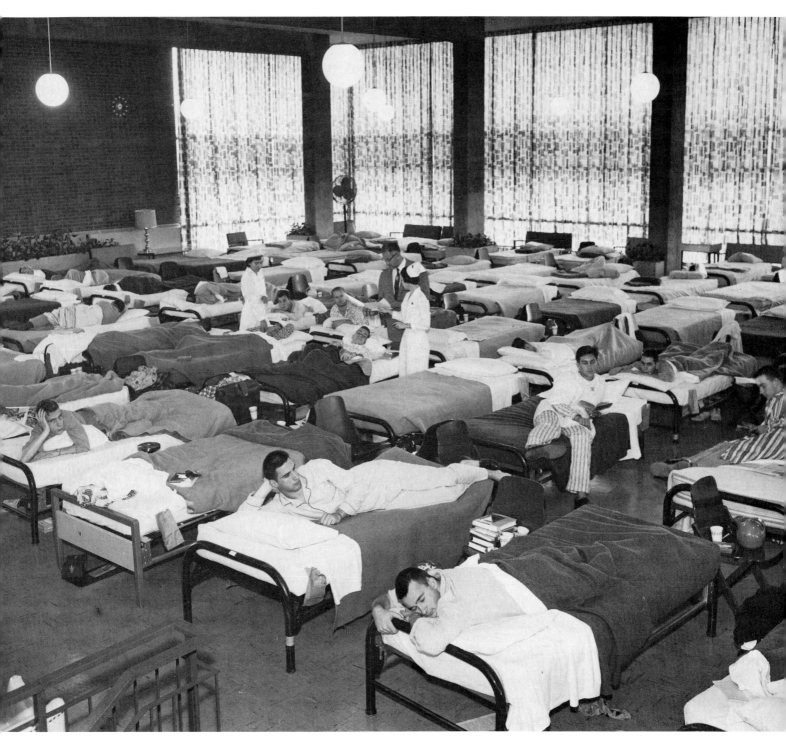

▼
RIVER DORMS, LATE 1950S
The men's college greatly increased its dormitory and classroom space with the completion of the river dorms in 1956 (the two floors of basement classrooms in each building are referred to as "the tombs" in student argot). The dorms are named for Theodorus Jacobus Frelinghuysen, a prominent Dutch clergyman in the early eighteenth century (the spirit of his great grandson, Theodore F. Frelinghuysen, president of Rutgers, 1850–1861, had to settle for a road named after him on the Busch campus); Jacob Rutsen Hardenbergh, president of Queen's College, 1785–1790; and William Henry Campbell, president of Rutgers, 1862–1882.

▼
DEMOLITION
Demolition along Bartlett Street, 1962, in preparation for the building of the student center. The location is now a parking lot.

KILMER OAK

The poet Joyce Kilmer was born and raised in New Brunswick and went to Rutgers between 1904 and 1906 (but graduated from Columbia). The popularity of his sentimental poetry was enhanced when he died young on the Western Front in 1918. In the late 1960s a university official recommended against naming the land on which Livingston was located the Kilmer Campus, on the grounds that Kilmer was "not a respectable poet" and the name would be an "insult" to the English department. He soon apologized for the comment, and the university came to terms with the name. The Kilmer Oak, 70 feet high and 110 feet across, stood between the agricultural college and Helyar woods. It was supposed to have inspired Kilmer's best-known poem, "Trees," written in 1913. The tree began to die in the 1950s and was cut down as a safety precaution—amid much lamentation—in 1963. Much of its wood has been turned into memorabilia.

TREES

I think that I shall never see
A poem lovely as a tree.

A tree whose hungry mouth is prest
Against the earth's sweet flowing breast;

A tree that looks at God all day,
And lifts her leafy arms to pray;

A tree that may in Summer wear
A nest of robins in her hair;

Upon whose bosom snow has lain;
Who intimately lives with rain.

Poems are made by fools like me,
But only God can make a tree.

▲
The poem.

▶
The tree, date of photo unknown.

"I think that I shall never se
A poem lovely as a tree."
— Joyce Kilmer

CAMDEN CAMPUS
The College of South Jersey originated as a law school, and an undergraduate college developed to support it in the early twentieth century. In 1950 it became part of Rutgers.

► A planning model for the expansion of Rutgers-Camden, 1963.

▼ The Ayer building, a mansion completed in 1869, was the first home of the college and is now the business office.

Newark Campus

Rutgers-Newark has a history similar to Rutgers-Camden, for it is based on the Newark Law School and a collection of private colleges—the Dana group—founded in the early twentieth century.

◄◄ In 1937 the Newark "campus" was the old Ballantine Building in the industrial downtown.

◄ View from the roof of the Ballantine Building, 1937.

▼ The modern Newark campus under construction on urban-renewal land, 1966.

▼
PLANNER, 1961
A planner for the university, Dr. Edward Wilkens, with a model of room furnishings and floor plans for the new dorms at University Heights, 1961.

UNIVERSITY HEIGHTS CAMPUS, 1964
In the 1950s, expansion at Rutgers-New Brunswick occurred on what is now called the College Avenue Campus and to a lesser degree at the Agricultural College. In the 1960s, Douglass began to cash in on newly available state and federal money, and the university built two brand-new campuses in Piscataway. University Heights became the science campus and represented the university's new emphasis on faculty research and on a much larger graduate program. From then on, the term "Rutgers students" would include a significant proportion of graduate students, with rather different orientations to college life than the undergraduates—and with especially attenuated ties to student community. From the undergraduate point of view, University Heights represented one more place to which they had to frequently travel on a daily basis for their science classes (unless they lived in the new dorms there, in which case they often had to travel elsewhere for their liberal arts classes). In the late 1960s, a plan was briefly entertained to move all of Rutgers College to University Heights, but enough money was never available for the move—and the move would have also involved leaving behind the historical heart of the college. In 1971, a wealthy New York investor who lived in Edgewater, New Jersey, Charles L. Busch, died and left about $10 million to Rutgers for biological research; in 1972, the University Heights campus was renamed Busch Campus in his honor. There was no known prior connection between Busch and Rutgers.

▼
In this 1964 aerial photo, Nelson Biological Labs was complete (lower left), as was Alcohol Studies (right of Nelson), the Wright-Reiman Labs (the vaguely traditional brick building and its companion which house the chemistry and geology departments), the engineering complex (the white buildings, upper right), and much of the physics complex (mid-right). The Tandem Accelerator was under construction, although the Library of Science and Medicine and the School of Pharmacy were yet unbuilt. The "temporary" faculty housing erected after World War II still survived and can be seen in the upper left background. Davidson dorm is also in the extreme upper left.

RUTGERS · THE STATE UNIVERSITY

◀

PROJECTIONS OF GROWTH, 1965
Projections of future growth, 1965, with President Mason Gross in attendance. In 1984 Rutgers (Newark and Camden included) had 29,739 full-time and 15,115 part-time students; the "evening" figure for 1984 (the University College totals) was 5,929.

▼

LIVINGSTON PLANNING
Livingston was the first of three small colleges proposed for construction on the so-called Kilmer tract in Piscataway—land donated to the university by the army from the base Camp Kilmer. Here in 1967, founding Dean Ernest Lynton points to a planning model for the proposed colleges. Of the three, only Livingston was completed. In the early 1970s, resources for the second were transferred to the new Cook College and plans for the third were shelved.

▶
ROUTE 18
The Route 18 construction and the new bridge (now called the Lynch Bridge) were originally proposed in the mid-1960s; due to controversy about their impact on the river dorms and the environment, however, they were not started until about 1980.

▼
GEORGE STREET, MID-1960S
Compared to the mildly prosperous nineteenth-century city, modern New Brunswick was a decaying town for three decades after World War II.

▼
New Brunswick, 1982

In the late 1970s, New Brunswick Tomorrow, a coalition of business and political leaders, began the revitalization of New Brunswick—renovating the shopping areas, tearing down whole blocks of old buildings, and making room for the buildings featured in this 1982 aerial photograph, the newly completed Johnson & Johnson World Headquarters and the Hyatt Hotel. It is interesting to compare this modern image to the 1845 lithograph (pp. 8–9) and the one from 1910 (pp. 42–43). Although New Brunswick can no longer celebrate its identity as a tidy, prosperous residential community, it hopes to do so in the future through revitalization. Most of the signs of its history, however, have been rooted out, with the river sealed behind the highway and the canal paved over (as well as the original site of Queen's College paved over, to the left of the tower near Albany Street in this photo). In another sense, however, the town has not changed drastically. Business and economic growth have always been at the core of its imagery: the railroads, the busy river and the new canal in 1845; smoky factories in 1910; and corporate capitalism and modern superhighways in 1982.

▶
Presidents

After World War II, Mason Gross was appointed the first provost at Rutgers, an administrative officer interposed between the president and the university. To manage the complexity of the modern university with seven campuses and a large graduate school, there are now three provosts and a number of vice-presidents; the president, once just the first among the faculty members, has become a relatively remote figure who sets goals, initiates planning, and deals with the state. This photo shows three postwar presidents of Rutgers at President Bloustein's inauguration in 1971. Left to right: Lewis Webster Jones, 1951–1959; Mason Gross, 1959–1970; Edward Bloustein, 1971–present.

SYMBOLS OF RUTGERS
There was no standard symbol of Rutgers in the late nineteenth century; different artists used different representations.

▲
A book stamp from 1918. The owl and the books remain from the nineteenth century (see illustration opposite); the sports equipment is new.

▲
This 1883 Commencement announcement is eclectic: Alma Mater, an owl (for wisdom), books, the initials *RC*, the lamp of learning, the college buildings, and a dawn scene with blackbirds singing in the cattails (the dawn of adult life?).

The coat of arms of Rutgers University, concocted in the 1960s. The upper left, upper right, and lower right quarters are from various European houses significant in the history of Rutgers. Only the lower left is native, symbolizing Rutgers as a land-grant institution.

The Scarlet Knight does not appear until about 1920.

▼
ADMINISTRATIVE OFFICERS, 1953
By the early 1950s the administration was becoming an increasingly impersonal force in the university. "These men," the 1953 yearbook caption said slightly apologetically, "often personally unknown to the students . . . [are] responsible for the smooth functioning of the college." They did not include the deans (of whom there were nine), the provost, or the president. The men's colleges then had an enrollment of about 6,000 students; none of these administrators worked for NJC. Today, the same photo would require a spread like the Old Queen's panorama (pp. 126–127); the University as a whole, with a student enrollment of 44,854, employs 332 executive, administrative, and management personnel. In the front row of this 1953 photo are (left to right): John L. Davis, Director of Housing; Edward H. Brill, Director of Purchases; Karl E. Metzger, Secretary (son of Dean of Men Fraser Metzger); Wallace S. Moreland, Director of Public Relations; George S. Kramer, Director of Admissions; and Albert S. Johnson, Comptroller. In the back row are: Courtney P. Brown, Superintendent, Buildings and Grounds; Bradford S. Abernethy, Chaplain; John R. Kirkwood, Director of Personnel and Placement; Donald F. Cameron, Librarian; Harry J. Rockafeller, Director of Physical Education (also shown in the 1928 football team photo, pp. 150–151); Edward Hurtado, Director of Student Health; and Luther H. Martin, Registrar.

Deans

The first dean at Rutgers was called Dean of the College but was really a dean of students. He was "Poppy" Van Dyke, appointed on a part-time basis in 1901. He was succeeded by Louis Bevier, David Fales, Fraser Metzger (in 1925, when dean of men and dean of the faculty became separate positions), Earl R. Rivers, Cornelius B. Boocock, Edgar Curtin, Howard Crosby, and currently, Stayton Wood. As the primary authority in contact with the students, the dean of men or dean of students inherited the personal, paternal role that all the faculty had had in the nineteenth century. Through the 1960s at least, the student yearbooks presented the dean as a man with a difficult job and regarded him with respect and affection. Since that time, the dean's relation to the students, like most relationships in the modern university, has become relatively impersonal and bureaucratic in nature.

▲
Fraser Metzger, 1928.

◄
Francis C. Van Dyke, in an early-twentieth-century photo.

Earl R. Silvers, holding a book he wrote.

Dean Stayton Wood, center, together with four members of his staff: left to right, Colleen Roach, residence counselor; Joan Carbone, associate dean; David Waldman, coordinator of residence life; and Betty Klindworth, assistant coordinator of residence life. In 1984 Wood's staff included two associate deans and five assistant deans.

By the time this 1958 photo was taken, the dean of men's office had expanded to include a number of officials. Sitting center is the dean, Cornelius Boocock. Sitting on the desk, right center, is the associate dean, Edgar Curtin, Boocock's successor as dean. Sitting on the left is Howard Crosby, assistant dean and Curtin's successor. At rear left is Thomas Leemon, whose book, *The Rites of Passage in a Student Culture* (about a Rutgers fraternity), is still in print. The fifth person is the campus proctor.

CLARK V. POLING

ROSS E. POWELL

DONALD C. REEVES

CLARK V. POLING '33

Schenectady, New York. Served in American Theater; Distinguished Service Cross, Chaplain, Army. Died aboard a troop ship torpedoed in North Atlantic February 2, 1943.

•

EMIL POTZER, JR. '43

Plymouth, Pennsylvania. Entered service May, 1943. Served in European Theater. Second Lieutenant, Army. Killed in action in France, June 15, 1944.

•

ROSS E. POWELL '45

Delanco, New Jersey. Entered service February 14, 1942. Served in European Theater. First Lieutenant, Infantry. Killed in action in Germany, November 24, 1944.

•

MILES V. REED '44

Trenton, New Jersey. Entered service May 1, 1942. Served in Pacific Theater. Second Lieutenant, Army Air Force. Killed in plane crash on Leyte, P. I., March 15, 1945.

•

DONALD C. REEVES '46

New Lisbon, New Jersey. Entered service September 1943. Served in European Theater. Private First Class, Infantry; Purple Heart. Killed in action in France, December 24, 1944.

•

GEORGE A. RENOUX '41

Milltown, New Jersey. Entered service July 1941. Served in European Theater. Major, Infantry. Died January 2, 1945 of wounds received in Belgium.

EMIL POTZER, JR.

MILES V. REED

GEORGE A. RENOUX

◀
WAR CASUALTIES
The campus became a virtual army camp in 1943 and 1944. This example from a twenty-nine-page section in the 1947 yearbook is a reminder of the death toll among Rutgers men.

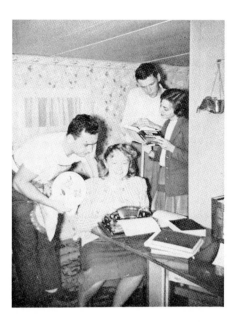

THE POSTWAR COLLEGE
For about five years after the war, the college enrolled large numbers of veterans.

▼
Students living in temporary barracks, probably at Raritan Arsenal, just after the war in 1946.

◀
The attitude of the post–World War II college toward its first married students seems a bit cloying today. This photo depicts the interior of a Hillside apartment. Hillside was a community of second-hand trailers installed at University Heights, not far from the stadium, for married veterans.

STUDENT LIFE

After the war, the sense of student community waned and groups of students were not photographed together as often as in earlier years (with the exception of fraternities and sports teams). Instead, in the increasingly individualistic postwar decades, the most common sort of student picture shows a few students doing something especially typical of the lighter side of student life. Many of the following photos were apparently taken by university publicists, who seem to have asked students to act out what they, the adults, considered emblematic college activities. The photographic perspectives of the students themselves might have been quite different, but such photos can probably be found only in privately-owned snapshot collections. (Alumni: please see p. 265, last paragraph.)

▶
STUDENT CAR

This young man evidently helped pay for his education by serving as a mobile billboard. The 1947 caption for the photo read: ''Roy Leury, Jr., with his 'carvertiser.'''

▼
AGGIES
Agricultural college students reinforce their stereotypes in a milk-drinking contest, 1950.

◀

TARGUM
Targum editors, 1950, trying very hard to look like a Hollywood version of the city room on a busy metropolitan newspaper.

▼

LIVING IT UP
Douglass College, about 1960.

► DANCE, 1957
An underclassmen's dance in the College Avenue Gym.

▼ STUDENT SOCIAL LIFE, 1950s
Rutgers men and NJC women, 1950s—a gender classic: the three women gaze into their dates' eyes. In all three couples, the man is the enclosing, almost faceless frame, the woman is the picture.

209

◄

STUDENT THEATRICALS
The wedding scene from *Allegro*, Little Theater, 1959.

▼

FRATERNITY BEER
A fraternity reinforcing its image, 1961.

Adult Education

After World War II, the university vastly expanded its adult education program, inaugurated in the 1930s, with branches of University College at Camden, Newark, and New Brunswick. A University College student from the early 1960s contrasted her adolescent college life with her return to University College as a married woman with two children—suggesting a modern image of Rutgers that is the common experience of many tens of thousands of students:

To me "college" [meant] cheers at football games, dances at fraternities . . . chapel bells in the twilight . . . But "college" also means a row of gaunt modern buildings along a sluggish river . . . a campus I have never explored on the outskirts of an ugly industrial town . . . masses of nameless, faceless students . . . [but] education brought with struggle and sacrifice into my adulthood [is] infinitely more rewarding than [that] absorbed in an ivory-tower atmosphere.

▼
In this 1959 photo from University College—Camden, the senior class is creating a little "college life" for itself, with a dinner-dance.

▲
The Engineering Student
This self-parody from 1963 shows more imagination than the standard university publicity shot.

▶
Intercampus Commuting
In the late 1950s, Douglass and Rutgers standardized their class hours, and the era of the traveling Rutgers student began in earnest. This schedule of an agricultural student from the class of 1960 was exhibited by the *Rutgers Alumni Magazine* as an example of a pretty rough schedule. It is easy, however, by modern standards: the guy had no classes at Livingston or Busch!

Goodman '60	Mon.	Tues.	Wed.	Thurs.	Fri.
1		PLANT PATHOLOGY Administration Bldg. Ag Campus		HISTOLOGY	
2		PLANT PHYSIOLOGY Lipman Hall Ag Campus	PHYS-LABS	HISTORY	
3 Lunch ④	ART Art House	ART Voorhees Hall	ABCS Van Dyck Hall	ART	PHYSICS
5	HISTOLOGY Douglass College	PLANT PATHOLOGY Administration Bldg. Ag Campus	PLANT PHYS	PLANT PATHOLOGY	HISTO
6	HISTORY Bishop House	PHYSICS Van Dyck Hall	PHYSIOLOGY Lipman Hall Ag Campus	PLANT PHYSIOLOGY	LAB LOBGY

▼
Student Scientist

Modern university photographers are not very imaginative at showing students. The great majority of the photos, despite their attempt to look informal, are as artificially constructed as the most formal late-nineteenth-century group pictures. A very common convention is to show an ethnically diverse group of men and women, smiling, in front of a university building or on a lawn. Another is to show the same set of youths, looking serious and intense, in class. Here is a third very common convention, of which there are several dozen examples among Rutgers publicity photos: To show a serious student, show a student scientist; to show a student scientist, put him or her in a white lab coat in front of scientific equipment. This is a food science photo from the early 1960s.

Rutgers College goes coed!

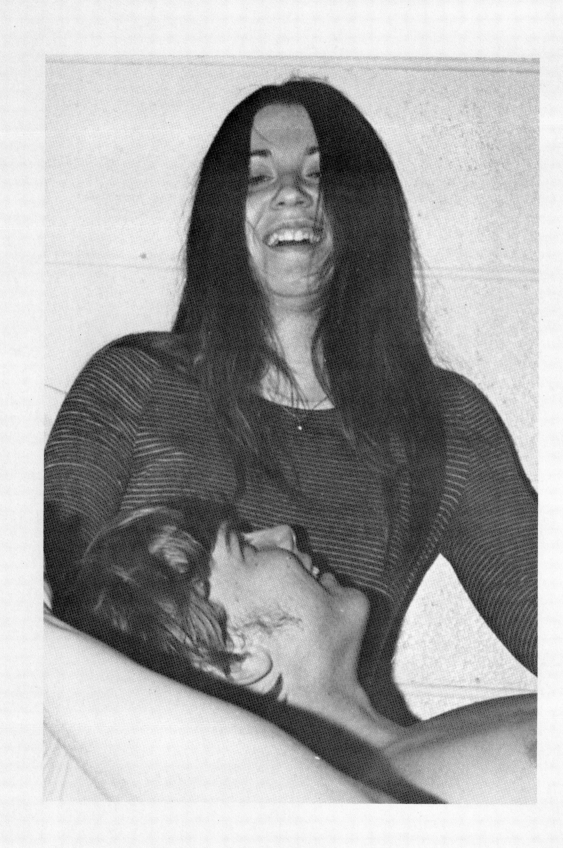

◀
COEDS

All of the colleges founded or incorporated into the Rutgers University system since World War II are coeducational, and the university as a whole currently educates slightly more women than men. The controversy over coeducation at Rutgers College developed again in the 1960s. The trustees and the dean of Douglass College were against it, but the faculty fought for it, and the Rutgers College Parents Association joined them at a critical juncture. The trustees changed their minds and approved coeducation, and the first female students arrived in 1972. Responding to student pressure, Rutgers quickly instituted coed dorms. A senior faculty member involved in the planning said that the college had expected a big uproar over coed dorms, but the late 1960s had apparently taken a toll on adult standards of traditional relationships between the sexes, and there was hardly a peep. In 1984 coed dorms are generally approved of by students in the college. Many of them argue that if men and women have to work closely in the real world, then they might as well learn how to get along in college.

FRESHMEN

College beanies or "dinks" survived at Rutgers until the late 1960s, and up to 1961 there was a little hazing (a "sophomore vigilante committee," for instance) and an interclass tourney. But the initiation of postwar freshmen was generally much less ritualized than it had been earlier in the century: a combination of the formal orientation program and informal student-to-student socialization in the dorms and fraternities.

▼
Dean Boocock giving a freshman orientation lecture in front of William the Silent in 1953.

"The Freshman Arriving"—a college publicity photo from the 1950s. The strict student-enforced dress rules of the earlier "procs" were not in evidence but the informal norms were fairly strict, teaching the incoming freshman to differentiate himself from noncollege youth. An upperclass columnist writing in the *Targum* in 1957 warned the freshman that the upperclassman "will be tall and Shetland-sweatered, with a belt on the back of everything he wears. He will look askance upon your spatterweave sportcoat and your framed, autographed pictures of Elvis Presley. He will introduce you to the saddle shoe and the desert boot, to the repp and fouland tie, to cords and chinos, to plaid belts and watchstraps. He will break to you gently that you will have to part with your beloved shock of black, flowing hair, and that cordovan is immensely superior to bluesuede."

The freshman parents' reception, 1961.

◀ Coats and ties were still occasionally worn by 1961, though Richard Zabriskie's may be more a matter of safe freshman dress.

▼ Freshmen with beanies and labels, in freshman English, NJC, 1950.

All three of these postwar photos of "typical" student living arrangements are obviously posed, but all are nevertheless (or possibly, therefore) very informative.

▶

The well-ordered, properly decorated college man's room, 1950s. The stolen signs were nothing new. Horace Hawes, a student at Rutgers in 1890, considered the acquisition of signs a basic right of the college student. A prize exhibit in one Rutgers student room in the late 1970s was a sign put up by the university to keep an important road open that read in part, "Don't even *dream* of stealing this sign!"

▼
Christmas dinner at Cooper Hall, Douglass College, 1950s.

▼
The disorderly look was as essential in this 1983 student room as the orderly look was in the 1950s—each photo is a summation of the student values of the time in which it was taken; both are exaggerations—the norm was less tidy than the 1950s photo and more tidy than the 1983 picture. In the 1980s, creative informality is a necessary contrast to the sterile order of the modern university. The caption for this yearbook photo says it all:

Large brick buildings plucked from the 1950's lie scattered around campus giving the impression that dorm life at Rutgers must be dull, cold, and rigid. Yet each year, without fail, thousands of students try to turn these ominous figures into a "slice of home." . . . [With a little creative decorating] you try to create a little corner where you can feel safe from the bureaucracy which awaits you outside.

▼

STUDENT LEXICON, 1980

By 1980, students in the large, relatively impersonal university had lost almost entirely the late-
nineteenth-century sense of Rutgers as a special
community that was somehow *theirs*. In this
sense, modern students most clearly resemble
early-nineteenth-century Rutgers students; they
still enjoy the "pleasures of student life," but
these can be experienced in very much the same
way at other colleges—Rutgers itself is not a
strong unit of identification. This 1980 student
lexicon is the smallest of the three shown in this
book, with only thirteen terms, mostly of 1960s
and 1970s origins; compare it with the one from
1874 (p. 63) and the one from 1920 (p. 131). No
terms have survived from the 1920 list.

▶

A STUDENT SCRAPBOOK, 1983

Personal scrapbooks were especially in vogue among students (and faculty members) between 1880
and 1920, and the many that survive in the Rutgers archives are a particularly valuable resource for
understanding personal views of college life during those years. Modern Rutgers students still keep
scrapbooks occasionally. This page is from one kept by a Rutgers freshman in 1983–1984 (even his
roommate was surprised to see it, a year later). It is a nicely organized, synthesizing image of modern
college life. "Secret Santa" is a popular dorm custom in which every student gives regular small pre-
Christmas presents to a partner—who does not know the identity of the giver. The nuclear explosion
paired with "academics" represents the freshman compiler's fear of what pledging a fraternity in his
first term might do to his grades.

Parlez-Vous Rutgers?

By BRUCE STOCKLER

Freshmen, transfers and other
students entering the University
are faced with a seemingly endless
barrage of difficulties:
overcrowded housing, long lines
for every conceivable facet of
academic or student life service, an
impossible parking situation and
other assorted dilemmas.

One of the lesser sticky spots in
this web of problems is the adjust-
ment to the many uniquely
Rutgers phrases employed by
veteran students.

The following is a thorough, but
not definitive, list of the sometimes
odd, often abusive and always
amusing "Rutgersisms":

•"The Banks" — From the
Alma Mater, "On the Banks of the
Old Raritan." The scenic, lovely
Raritan, which fraternity members
used to traverse unclad regularly,
might now catch fire if you drop a
cigarette into it.

•"Aggies" — A term that was
much more popular five years ago,
it refers to Cook College students,

because of their agricultural interests. It can be taken either an-
tagonistically or affectionately.

•"Guts" — Meaning any
Rutgers courses requiring little or
no real work, occasional class attendance at best, and which
guarantees a minimum grade of
'C'. Unofficial experts in this area
include *Targum* editors, most
fraternity upperclassmen and
graduate students with liberal arts
degrees.

•"The Rock" — Livingston
College's old and fading
nickname. Also known as the
Heights. Presumably named out of
bitterness over the college's isola-
tion from the main campus. It's
always windier here.

•"Throats" — Once thought to
be only a Rutgers phrase, it is now
in common use on the college cir-
cuit. The term is applied to those
students whose highest, and
perhaps only, priority during the
academic year is holing up in the
library to ensure a berth on the
dean's list.

Through blizzards, grain parties
and yes, even weekends, the
"throat" can be seen sneaking into
the library with a couple of sodas
and a bag of cheese Goldfish, complete with his/her calculator strap-
ped onto the belt and 108 pounds
of books stuffed into a knapsack.

•"The Libes" — The various
campus libraries where throats and
normal-type students do research,
sleep and study; Alexander is the
most notable, what with its reputation for deviant sexual behavior in
the bathrooms of the bottom floor.

•"The Barn" — The College
Ave. gymnasium. Dubbed as such
for its lurid, gaping appearance, it
either smells like one or, during

concerts, the people inside act like
animals.

•"Rippos" — And Dippos, Cip-
pos, Lippos, and Bippos, acronyms
or the post office boxes. Not much
else to say.

•"The Tombs" — The nether-
most floors of the river dorms used
after classes for studying purposes.
Beats overcrowded dorm lounges
and stuffy libraries.

•"Debbie Douglass" — An
alternately nasty and sarcastic
epithet bestowed upon the women
of one of America's great women's
colleges. Implying snobbery and a
practiced air of cool indifference,
the term was phrased by flustered
males during the mating season.

•"Passion Puddle" — The
Douglass pond that has inspired
countless moments of unabashed
romance. Actually, one of the mel-
lowest, most scenic spots on the
New Brunswick campus . . . if you
can ignore the grafitti-covered
parking deck that looms nearby.

•"Frat Rat" — A unisex term.
Greeks refer to women who frequent their social functions as
such, and women who don't make
a habit of attending frat parties use
the term to refer to the lustful
males they envision lurking above
with beer-in-hand, drooling.

•Last, and most important of
all, "The R.U. Screw" — The
seemingly very real, simultaneous-
ly subtle and brazen attempt by the
administration to render life here
difficult, if not miserable. Once
considered only a paranoia of the
student left, the term was used by
University administrators to argue
in favor of reorganization.

**Bruce Stockler is a *Targum* news
editor and one of the unofficial experts on "guts".**

The Throat

What College is REALLY Like

I WANT YOU

To **Go** to the

bi\/\y

idol

show

with _Me_ !

Pre~~gn~~ancy

'83' ~~DEMICS~~

R~~UTG~~ERS

TKE

RU
Screw
3 WRONG
Classes !

college town

Secret Santa

Owner
of a
Lonely Heart♥

12 **Drinkin' buddies.**

MAKE IT
PERSONAL

rutgers 17⚕66 targum

Vol. 102, No. 1   NEW BRUNSWICK, N.J.   THURSDAY, SEPTEMBER 10, 1970

Perspective

The Freshman Unhandbook

By JEFF LADERMAN

To orient the incoming freshman class, the Student Government Association and various deans' offices publish a handbook, and to quote from this years' edition, "Yawn, another official publication. ZZZzzz..."

Every year its editors make some attempt to unofficialize the handbook and so the end produce becomes an unofficial-looking (so that the students might trust it) yet hopelessly official institution.

Probably the most subjective essay collection anyone could compose would be on a living experience, such as college life. There are innumerable views on life at Rutgers, and so to present another perspective and alternative to the "official dope", Targum brings you the Freshman Unhandbook.

Curricula (p.8)

When the handbook defines "liberal arts education as a 'process of discriminating judgement, judicious descernment, etc.," its putting you on. The libbies' life is no ivory tower-love of learning existence.

The realities of the Rutgers College usually means "getting by" or the best possible cume with the least possible work. The grading structure has done an effective job of stifling, real intellectual pursuit. A "1" or "2" in a course is more important than what you've learned.

Although some efforts have been makde by certain departments (through pass/fail systems) to reorient freshman courses away from the grade to the material, the overwhelming experience for the majority of Rutgersmen is the competitive rat race—where cume is God and you only have to learn enough to get a certain grade.

Some courses have grade quotas (with a built-in failure rate) while in others your work will be in the hands of a vengeful grad students instead of the professor who's teaching the course. It won't be long before you've discovered the absurdity of the grading system and how it keeps you from getting an education.

Academic advisors (p. 16)

These guys are instructors who also advise, have little time for advising, and even less interest in it. For academic problems, you're much better off seeking your preceptor, or an upperclassman's advice—he's probably had a similar problem or knows someone who has.

The advisors in Milledoler Hall only know you from your file they hold in front of them while you're visiting them. If you ask them about a course they'll look up the answer in the catalogue, which you could do yourself. In most cases, the advisor can best service you by signing your program card at registration time.

Federated College Plan (p.2)

The Federated College Plan is a shrewd blueprint devised by some bureaucrats in Old Queens to propogate provincialism and tradition. This plan keeps Rutgers all male (despite that its been almost two years since the faculty and students have overwhelmingly endorsed a coed Rutgers College.) keeps Douglass forever female, and encourages animosity and friction instead of cooperation between the colleges.

The bureaucratic hassles involved are amazing. For example, in one course there can conceivably be students from three grading systems. For the departments, the plan means duplicating each other rather than cooperation. Economically, it would be best to offer one introductory psychology course for all freshmen, instead of one for Douglass, another for Rutgers, and still another for Livingston, etc. Departments could save money by eliminating duplication, but because of the FCP, they don't.

(Continued on Page 6)

Modern student satire of the institution is not so rich as it once was, probably because students are not as interested in the institution as they once were. At Rutgers College, one of its few regular modern forms is the *Mugrat*, the annual parody of the *Targum*, so cleverly produced that it regularly tricks the unwary into paroxysms of emotion over such "news" as the imminent collapse of the river dorms into the Raritan, the faculty calling a wildcat strike, and the health center supplying defective contraceptives to the students.

◄

In 1970, under the impact of heightened student political involvement, most vestiges of the older way of life were erased by the students themselves. This is the first page of a satire of the older, college-produced, freshman handbook.

▲
Academic cynicism secondhand—"Doonesbury," from the 1972 yearbook.

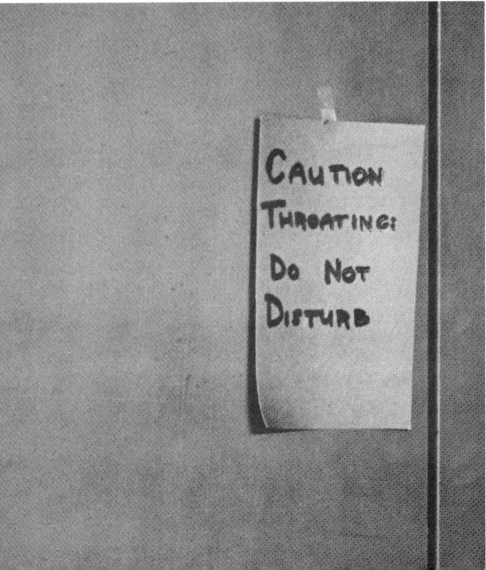

◄
ANTI-INTELLECTUALISM
Modern student anti-intellectualism is not nearly so strident as it was in the late-nineteenth-century college. Most students now at Rutgers need to do well in school in order to meet their career goals; very few go into the family business after college. In the late 1970s, good students were generally admired by their peers so long as they appeared to be "normal" human beings as well. The "throat" (short for *cutthroat*) was the 1970s equivalent of the old "bootlicker"—the student overly concerned with high grades and faculty favor. The term "throat" seems to be unique to Rutgers and does not seem to be more than twenty years old. It is apparently dying out and being replaced by a variety of high-school-derived terms.

CHANGING STUDENT TRADITIONS

Howard Crosby recently remembered an occasion in 1959 when he first realized that the job of the dean of men was changing. As an assistant dean, he was called out one night to stop a water fight between Delta Upsilon and Ford Hall; local residents had called the police. After convincing the police to leave, he walked out on the street and was immediately surrounded by students. Every time he tried to say something, the students applauded so he could not be heard. Finally he mentioned that the Military Ball was coming soon: any fraternity member who did not leave soon would find his house forbidden to hold a house party. Crosby was alone, and he was worried that the students would throw water on him—"A fuming dean drenched with water would have done no good"—but they dispersed. It was the first time that Crosby had felt some trepidation about his ability to do his job. He still had the power in those days to enforce his threat immediately, but he realized the days of Fraser Metzger, when the students would have dispersed the moment the dean appeared, were over.

▼
This photo shows a toilet-paper fight in 1973.

Activism

Student activism did not begin at Rutgers in the 1960s; it began in the 1930s when—under the impact of the Great Depression—college students became more seriously concerned with social and political questions and with college as an institution. There were further instances of student activism at Rutgers in the 1940s and in the late 1950s, when the first demonstrations occurred. The image of the demonstrating student rather than the older image of the fun-loving student became popular in the late 1960s, at Rutgers as elsewhere. Many other groups also began to employ the demonstration as a means for visibility in a seemingly blind bureaucratic world. In the early 1970s, for instance, Campus Patrol demonstrated in front of Old Queen's to be upgraded to Rutgers University Police, a change that the university quickly endorsed.

▼
Fraternity men from Alpha Gamma Rho returning from a demonstration in Trenton protesting financial cutbacks, 1957.

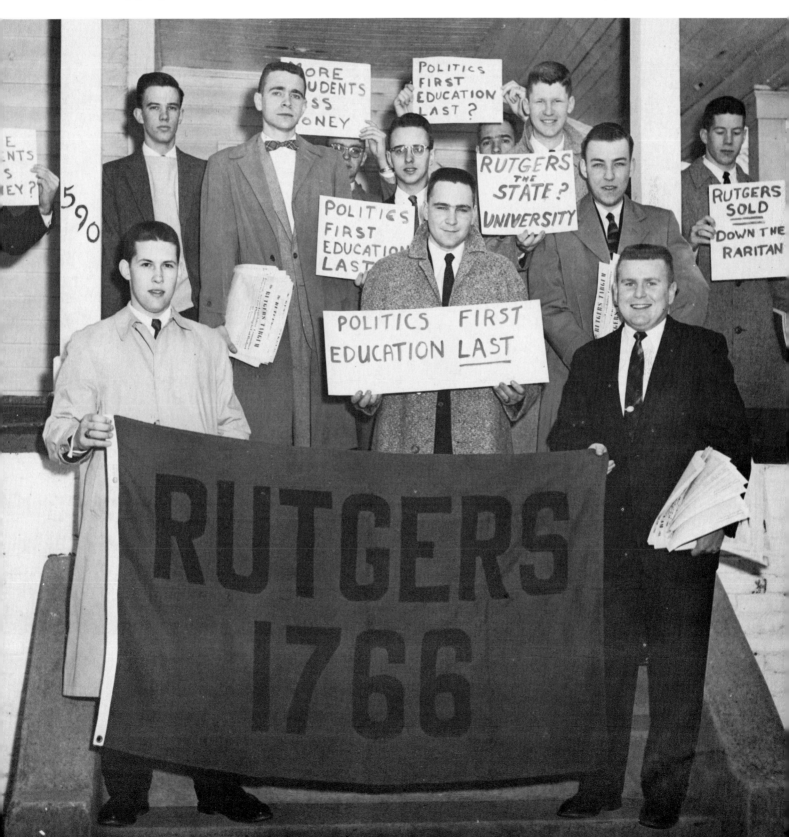

▶
Kennedy-era activism: a publicity photo showing a student from Nigeria listening to the plans
of Russell Kroeker, Rutgers '63, who after graduating hoped ''to build Nyasaland's first radio
station.'' In 1967 Kroeker listed himself on an
alumni form as managing director and president
of Nzeru Radio Company, Blantyre, Malawi (the
postcolonial name of Nyasaland).

▼
Student demonstrations in favor of the state
bond issue, around 1958.

In February 1969, black students protesting institutional racism took over buildings at Camden and Newark. On the advice of a student-faculty committee, Rutgers College canceled classes for three days of symposia on black issues in the college (which then had approximately 50 black students). Here the black student spokesman Randy Green, a freshman, speaks to a convocation of over 2,000 students and faculty in the College Avenue Gym. He is remembered as an "incredible orator." Rutgers Dean Arnold Grobman sits behind him. Sitting left of Grobman, hands on knees, is David Burns, class of 1970, chairman of the Student-Faculty Community Action Committee—and in 1984, assistant vice-president for student life policy and services at Rutgers.

A faculty meeting in the gym during the same period. Richard McCormick, center, was appointed chair of a select student-faculty committee on the issues of the day; Mark Singley, right, was also on the committee. Here the faculty discusses the black demands (most of which are remembered as reasonable and most of which were acted upon positively), while the students listen from the balcony—having only recently been given the right to attend faculty meetings.

THE ANTIWAR MOVEMENT

The heart of the late-1960s, early-1970s college youth movement was the nationwide protest against the war in Vietnam. In early May, 1972, students at Rutgers—like American college students virtually everywhere else, and with considerable faculty sympathy—organized actions to protest President Nixon's decision to escalate the war by mining the harbors of North Vietnam.

▼

Around May 10th, some Rutgers students took over the Army ROTC headquarters for about a day, and then left voluntarily. In this photo, members of what was then called the campus patrol guard the building against another occupation. In the days before the campus patrol was professionalized, following the model of other police, their attire looked like a cross between the dress of adult collegiate authorities and the uniform of riot police.

▼

On May 12th, a group of students protested the mining of Haiphong harbor by sitting down on the railroad tracks in the New Brunswick station and blocking commuter trains for an hour and a half. When a reporter asked one participant why the students didn't sit on other, higher-speed inner tracks, he responded sensibly that they didn't "want to get squished." While 150 students demonstrated on the platform, and some faculty looked on, 18 students were arrested (although quickly released).

▶
A RECENT DEMONSTRATION
The demonstration mode of protest was not forgotten after the 1960s. Here, students demonstrate against "reorganization" in 1981.

◀
CAMPUS SECURITY
The older, smaller, more elitist university could easily keep track of who belonged to it and who didn't. In the late 1960s, however, as student dress codes changed to resemble those of other youths, and as the university expanded and became more closely linked to a troubled urban society, its boundaries became more permeable and more problematic to enforce. The result was the developing issue of campus "security" and the expansion of the campus police (also useful against student "disorders"). Bomb scares were epidemic for a time. *Rutgers Alumni Monthly* reported that there had been 21 in the first month of 1971 alone. The photo is from a 1971 *Scarlet Letter*.

" You won't find any ivy covered walls here."

LIVINGSTON

Livingston College was the most thoroughgoing recent attempt by the university to provide for a sense of student community—and student power—within the modern institution. From its opening in 1969, it was a hotbed of excitement and crisis.

▼

The first issue of the Livingston student newspaper, which was preceded by a mimeographed newsletter.

►

An example of Livingston political expression, 1979.

◄

Though Livingston resembled older American colleges in its small size, it was fervently anti-traditional, as is shown in a 1974 yearbook photo and caption.

the livingston *MEDIUM*
vol. one, no. two
october 8, 1970

Are we (still) going to survive? And how?

By ROY KIRLEY

September 30, 1970. A day for Livingston students to remember? Maybe, maybe not. An emergency meeting of the general student body took place that night at 7:30.

The meeting was chaired by Debbie Smith. The purpose of the meeting, as stated by Debbie in her opening remarks, was to discuss the intimidation and harassment of certain students. This was to be discusssed in the context of Livingston's survival. Debbie also spoke of administrative inadequacies, particularly in leadership.

Lack of regulations

Dean Lynton was the next to speak. He assumed the responsibility for the lack of regulations on intimidation and harrassment, and then stated that neither "will be tolerated." Dean Lynton also stated that any group wanting to live together would be allowed a single house, but not a complete unit, to do so.

At the completion of Dean Lynton's speech, Debbie assumed the chair. What was to follow was somewhat chaotic and confusing. The purpose of this article is to reproduce that meeting without some of the emotionalism and bull, which prevailed at the meeting, and get down to what the people really had to say. This was done by asking the various people and organizations present at the meeting to express themselves by means of a written statement.

Groups, individuals speak

The main factions and students who spoke at that meeting, specifically Debbie Smith, Dean Lynton, OBU, Fred Thorne, UPRS, Fourth World Coalition, Nearo Williams and an unnamed white student were invited to address their statements to these basic questions:

Lee Weiner Interview
"It's not going to be my revolution; it's going to be our revolution"

By PETER BRANN

Equipped with a tape

return home again. Next month he hopes to buy a car. He is teaching two courses (Social Problems and Deviance, and Organized Social Movements and

good place to work but I don't know if it's a good place to be a student. There's plenty of good reasons to be at a university campus. There are a lot of things

Are The Livingston Woods Angry? ★ Mesthene on Livingston Image ★ Basic Skills ★

Freedom Of Speech

Sanitized Transcripts

Housing Priorities

LUT

NAB suite held in black protest

LUCY STORE

Rally peaceful but no deans attended

NEW DEAN WANTED

continue struggle

In Search of Unity

Silence from Dean

300 students sit in at Rutgers library

's contr... ...ER STUDENTS ...ts p...
...Livingston dean

CAMPUS PROTESTS U. OF TEXAS HEAD

New President Is Opposed by Faculty and Students

Reaffirm Livingston

"With me, there was no conscience, nothing involved. It was a job. I never lost one night's sleep over it."

FUNERAL RITES
for
LIVINGSTON

Resurrect the Spirit

...story...

...nce upon a time, there was ...bunch of people who were ...tuck in a hole.

attempts were made by various individuals to get out of the hole...

such as desperate arm flapping...

...jumping...

...meditation and levitation

This went on for hundreds of years, until they had tried everything except helping each other out ...

...so they helped each other out

TUESDAY OCT. 21 7:30 P.M.
TILLETT LOUNGE

Minority   Cutbacks

Centralization

★ Is The End In Sight For Puerto Rican Studies? ★

MODERN STUDENT SENSIBILITIES

Late nineteenth-century *Scarlet Letters* were entirely student-produced, and their organization and contents presumably expressed student priorities (fraternities, sports, student clubs, satires, and reflections on "college life," with only incidental mentions of academics). The modern yearbook is harder to interpret, since its format is apparently imposed by the nationally based companies that specialize in its production. Most modern yearbooks, however, contain more interesting student-designed subsections. These photos are taken from a spread on Student Life in the 1982 *Scarlet Letter*, and suggest the common undergraduate experiences with Rutgers as a large, bureaucratic institution—the range of experiences partly covered by the global student metaphor, "the RU Screw." Student-written captions for this spread include: "mystery bus ride to nowhere"; "close encounters of a long line"; and "commons cuisine ain't like Mom used to make." The evolving parking regulations were part of the "screw" affecting faculty and administrators as well as students.

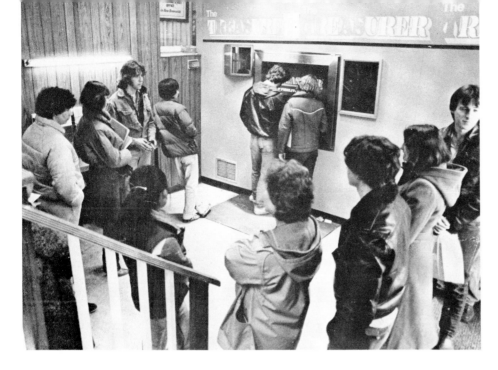

Another Rutgers Man— on the way

Remember when it was you standing there? How you squirmed when
your father saw that one bad report
card. You're glad now that he made
you buckle down — grateful that you
were able to go on to one of the country's finest universities.

Naturally, you want to be just as
farsighted about your own son's
future. So now that he's one year
closer to college — wouldn't it be
wise to call your Massachusetts

Mutual man and discuss the best insurance plan for his education?

*And since this is the time for report
cards and review, perhaps you should re-
evaluate your own career.* Are you as far
along as a man of your ability should
be? For example, are you earning as
much as $13,500 a year? That was the
1960 average income of 630 represen-
tatives who have been with the
Massachusetts Mutual Life Insurance Company five years or longer.

They are men like you — men
chosen for their fine education and
background. All received thorough
training and earned while they
learned. Now they are established in
a career that uniquely combines inde-
pendence with stable income — plus
the security of group insurance and
retirement benefits.

If you would like to know more
about this opportunity, write for a
free copy of "A Selling Career".

MASSACHUSETTS MUTUAL *Life Insurance Company*

SPRINGFIELD, MASSACHUSETTS · ORGANIZED 1851

To every roommate about to become a friend.

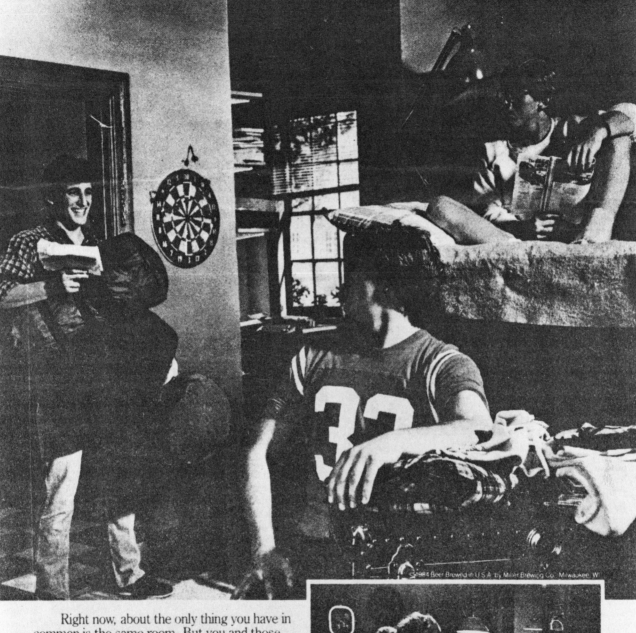

Right now, about the only thing you have in common is the same room. But you and those strangers who moved in with you are going to crack a lot of books and burn a lot of midnight oil together.

You're going to discover the people behind the nametags, the ones inside the roommates. And who knows? Before the term is over, your roommates may very well turn out to be good friends.

To each of you we say, let it be Löwenbräu.

Löwenbräu. Here's to good friends.

FRATERNITIES

Fraternities ran counter to the strongly egalitarian values of most college students in the 1960s, and Rutgers fraternity memberships dropped to a low—less than 25 percent of the student body in the 1970s. Since then, however, they have held their own, and a new sorority system has developed. In the impersonality of the modern university, they are havens of friendship and sociability. The tone of the modern fraternity appears to be determined more by the norms of general American youth culture (music, partying, dress) than by concepts of a highly distinctive sort of "fraternity man," as in the 1950s and earlier. Notably missing is the former emphasis on social graces and elaborate ritual. Recent preppie styles, however, may indicate a return to the older traditions.

▼
The candlelight service, Greek Week, 1952. A member of each house lit a candle on the altar of Kirkpatrick Chapel, a fraternity tradition that is long gone from Rutgers.

▼
Theta Chi still had a housemother in 1961.

▲
Modern fraternity youth in formal garb, after a pledge banquet.

◄
About 1966 the fraternities argued that they could finance improvements to their houses better if they no longer had to support the financial burden of a housemother; the college authorities (who were phasing out in loco parentis elsewhere in student life in any case) agreed. Not only is the housemother gone from this 1966 Zeta Psi photo, so is the old formal pose. Fraternity photos at Rutgers after the mid-1960s recapture a visual interest they last had in the late nineteenth century, after fifty years of stiffly posed rows of well-dressed young men.

▶
A page from the scrapbook of a modern Gamma Phi Beta member. As in the 1930s, the paddle remains symbolically central. The memorabilia at the bottom are from the *Targum*, examples of a student genre also found in nineteenth-century scrapbooks and elsewhere: the sentimental, opaque public communication, meaningful to only a few.

▼
Modern sorority etiquette.

DELTA MU CHAPTER

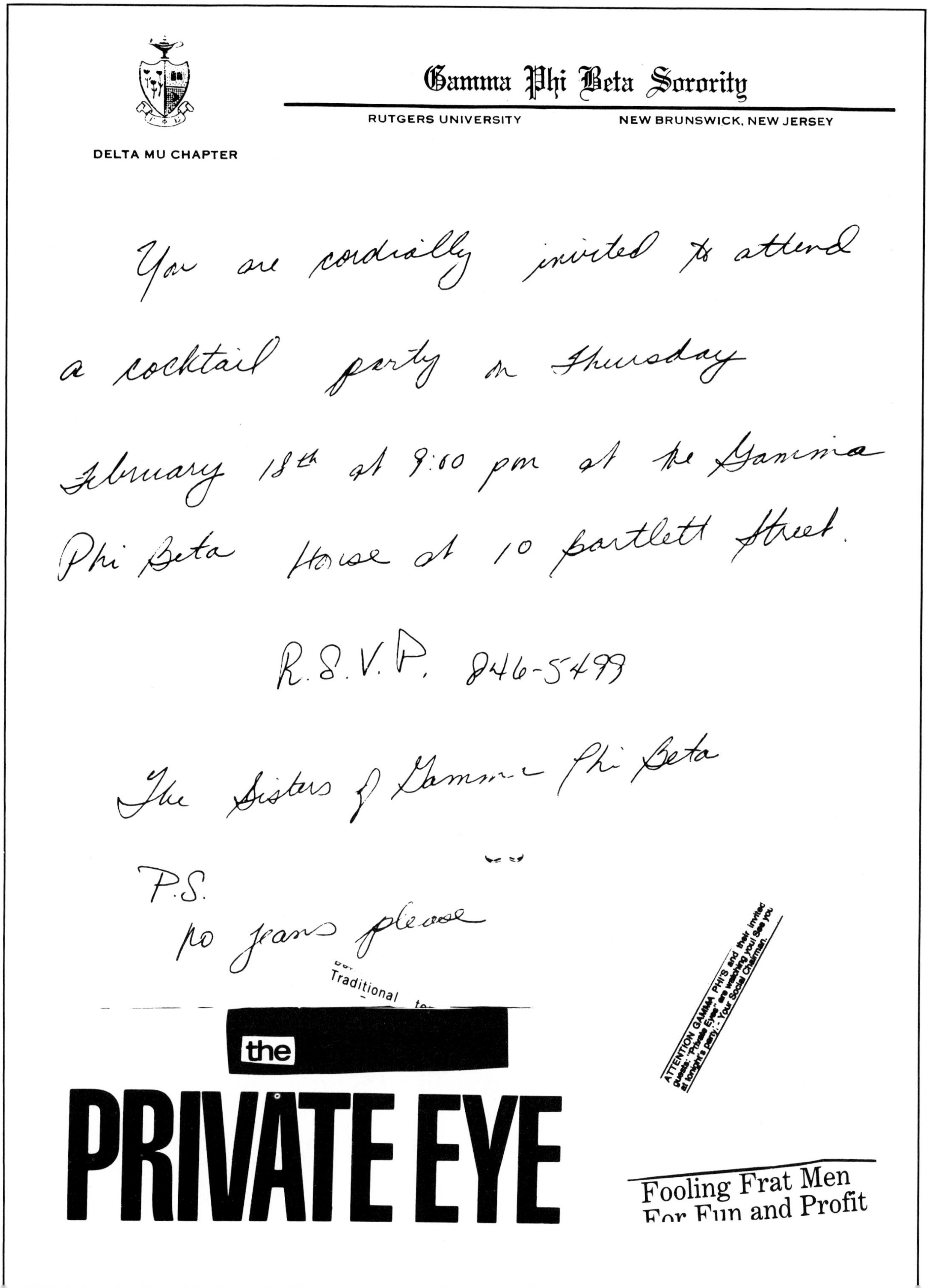

Gamma Phi Beta Sorority

RUTGERS UNIVERSITY NEW BRUNSWICK, NEW JERSEY

You are cordially invited to attend a cocktail party on Thursday February 18th at 9:00 pm at the Gamma Phi Beta House at 10 Bartlett Street.

R.S.V.P. 846-5499

The Sisters of Gamma Phi Beta

P.S.
no jeans please

Traditional

the

PRIVATE EYE

ATTENTION GAMMA PHI'S and their invited guests: "Private Eyes" are watching you! See you at tonight's party. - Your Social Chairman.

Fooling Frat Men
For Fun and Profit

O GAMMA PHI BETA Sorority - Once again ou've got the best looking pledges and sisterhood n campus. We can't wait to get a closer look on the 8th. An admiring Fraternity.

O JIM K. From Chi Psi, I'm looking forward to hursday night at Gamma Phi Beta. See you there.

O THE SISTERS of Gamma Phi Beta, Thank you or accepting me as I am and encouraging me to

GAMMA PHI BETA means having sisters that you know and love. Let's go SPRING PLEDGES. Julie - you're the best big sis - Karen.

GINGER - Loving you and GAMMA PHI BETA has and will always be a deeply emotional, beautiful experience for me. Love, Melinda.

SANDY, A sister is forever. Thanks for being a wonderful one to me. GAMMA PHI BETAS We'll always be. Eilene.

COLLEEN, I'll try my best to follow in your footsteps as Gamma Phi's S.F. Queen - Wish me Luck - Sue.

TO MY S.B.S. - Thanks for showing me that GAM-MA PHI BETA is the Best - Love, Your S.L.S.

SANDY MENDEZ - I'll always be grateful to Gam-ma Phi for giving me such a great little sister! Love Always, Sue.

EILENE, Being your sister in Gamma makes everything so much better. Lo Sandy.

Personals

Football

Like so much else in Rutgers student culture, varsity football has become increasingly alienated from student life; seventy-five years ago students actually ran the team. Since then, a much smaller proportion of the student body has actively participated in varsity sports. Most of the hard-worked student athletes who play on the varsity teams today live together on distant parts of the campus; the average student rarely knows any of them personally. The nature of collegiate fandom has also changed. Late-nineteenth and early-twentieth-century Rutgers students supported the Rutgers team, under the "do or die" (and it was often die) motto. Now, as with other professional sports in our media-dominated society, Rutgers teams usually generate student interest only when they win. The varsity football record since World War II has been up and down, with strong teams in 1947 and 1948, undefeated teams in 1961 and 1976, and apparently improving prospects in 1984.

◄
Intramural Football
Intramural football, allowing the average student's participation in the sport, has continued to be popular at Rutgers. A late-1950s intramural touch game, in a field behind the gym (now a parking lot).

◄
The Rutgers-Princeton Series
The Rutgers-Princeton game has been the oldest rivalry in American football. Traditionally, Princeton always won. After the first Rutgers victory in 1938, however, Rutgers began to win occasionally, as in this 1959 game, which shows Rutgers students attacking the goalposts after an 8–6 Rutgers victory. In the 1970s, as Rutgers upgraded its football program, Princeton pulled out of the series. It was apparently reasonable for an Ivy League team to cease competing with a "big time team," but it was an ironic decision from a Rutgers point of view. In the late nineteenth and early twentieth centuries, tiny Rutgers had for years annually offered itself up to what was then, effectively, "big-time" Princeton.

◄◄
Football player, 1943
By 1943, Rutgers varsity football players wore hard helmets rather than the original leather helmets, but the face mask had not yet been developed.

▼ Women and Football

The caption for this 1969 photo, part of the same Rutgers-Princeton centennial celebration, reads: "Barbara Specht, Texas Technological College junior and National Football Centennial Queen, learns that a scrimmage is no place for a lady." In 1984, intramural football competition rules for Rutgers College dorms required that each team had to contain at least two women or it would forfeit (in actual play, however, the women—some of whom were talented, experienced athletes—had a difficult time getting their male teammates to let them handle the ball).

▶ A Battleworn Player

Late nineteenth-century football developed as a tough, "manly" sport, in which bodily protection was minimal and injuries were common. Late twentieth-century collegiate football is as tough, although in different ways. The modern player is protected by an armory of equipment as elaborate as that of any medieval knight, and by advanced physical training methods and sports medicine. However, the equipment of the opponent is also a new weapon, and the opponents themselves are bigger, stronger and more specialized every year.

▼ The Football Centennial

In 1969, Rutgers and Princeton celebrated the centennial of the first football game. Here, student athletes re-create the "original football game" on a field at University Heights. The players are mildly authentic down to the waist; the footgear and the football are modern. Compare this photo to the painting of the original football game, chapter 2 (p. 75).

▼
Rutgers-Virginia, 1981
A splendid photo of a Rutgers-Virginia game at
the Meadowlands, won by Rutgers 3−0. Played
on synthetic turf, in clean uniforms, in a stadium
thirty miles from the main campus, the look of
the game is almost indistinguishable from a professional football game.

◀
DICK ANDERSON
In 1984, Rutgers recommitted itself to big-time
football, the state of New Jersey kicked in $3
million in capital improvements for the program,
and the team recruited a dynamic new head
coach from Penn State, Dick Anderson.

▲
VARSITY COACHING STAFF, 1982
This official photo of the 1982 varsity football coaching staff shows: (front row) Bill Speranza, offensive
coordinator; Frank Burns, Rutgers '48 and head coach 1973–1983; Earle Mosely, defensive backfield
coach; George DeLeone, defensive coordinator; (back row) Dick Curl, receiver coach; Greg Gigantino,
defensive line coach; Bob Guarini, offensive backfield coach; James Taigia, offensive line coach; and
Mike Jacobs, defensive end coach.

BASKETBALL

Basketball started at Rutgers in the early twentieth century, but few teams attained regional or national prominence until the 1960s.

▶

JIM VALVANO

Jim Valvano, shown here (right) as a student in his senior year, 1967, was a scrappy Rutgers player known for his defense on a team that went 22-7 and finished third in the NIT. He was also known as a student wit and cutup, whose extracurricular activities included pledging four different fraternities ("free lunches at every one!"). He has gone on to a highly successful college coaching career, leading an uneven North Carolina State team to the National Championship in 1983, an achievement which John Wooden, a coaching immortal, termed one of the "two finest NCAA tournament coaching jobs" he had ever seen.

▶
WOMEN'S BASKETBALL
The women's varsity, or the "Lady Knights," has been as successful as the men's team recently. June Olkowski, shown here in a 1978 photo, starred on the 1981–1982 team that won the national championship in the Association of Intercollegiate Athletics for Women (since merged with the NCAA).

◀
MEN'S VARSITY, 1976
Coach Tom Young (far left) and members of the great 1976 varsity men's team that reached the quarterfinals of the NCAA national championship, here accepting the Eastern College Athletic Conference cup of that year. The players, left to right: Phil Sellers, Mike Dabney, Mike MacDonald (holding|up index finger), Sylvester Allen, Jeff Kleinbaum and Hollis Copeland.

▶
CREW

Crew, together with football and baseball, was part of the original student athleticism which developed at Rutgers—and in every other American college—in the 1860s. Because boats and facilities were expensive and the Rutgers athletic funds were so low, however, crew lapsed in the late nineteenth century, and was revived only in the 1930s. The greatest moment in Rutgers rowing occurred in 1952. Crew coach Charles Logg wanted to enter Rutgers in the Helsinki Olympics, but his eight-man team was not strong enough that year. He decided to spend his own money on a two-man shell, putting his son, Charles Logg, Jr., in one seat and a talented freshman, Thomas Price, in the other. The two young men practiced together for only three months, and then left for Helsinki. Incredibly, they took the gold medal in the "pairs-without-coxswain" event—an event never before won by Americans. This photo shows them after their victory, Price left, Logg right.

▼
LACROSSE

Lacrosse is another Rutgers sport with nine-teenth-century roots. Recent teams have had some national success. The 1984 team, for instance, reached the final eight in the NCAA championships. In this 1984 photo, Rutgers attack-man Ed Trabulsy heads for the Hofstra goal.

▼
MR. MAGOO
In the 1960s the most famous alumnus of Rutgers was probably the cartoon character Mr. Magoo. For years, the university wondered why. Had one of Magoo's creators or Jim Backus, the "voice" of Mr. Magoo, attended Rutgers? The answer turned out to be neither of the two. Mr. Magoo went to Rutgers simply because—according to a Hollywood informant—his creators wanted him to be "a college alumnus who was still fired up with the old school spirit [and they felt] that Rutgers was the embodiment of the 'old school tie' in America." The old quasi–Ivy League image of Rutgers lives on, increasing according to distance from New Jersey, and apparently peaking in southern California. Magoo is a recent expression of the "I'd Die for Dear Old Rutgers" phenomenon.

ALUMNI

Many of the alumni of an older, smaller, simpler Rutgers have remained amazingly loyal to the new, enormous institution, trooping to New Brunswick every five years for parades and reunions. It will be interesting to see if the university can maintain the same loyalty among students of the modern, less-personal university when they become alumni.

First Annual Alumni Day Dinner
Rutgers University—University College
Essex House—Newark, N.J. June 5, 1949

▼
An alumni dinner for University College-Newark in 1948—banquet camera still in use.

The Class of 1938 at their twenty-fifth reunion in 1963. Richard P. McCormick, University Historian and editorial consultant for this book, is sitting at the left end of the table wearing a jacket and no hat.

Members of the Class of 1940, which made a generous contribution to the funding of this book, celebrate their older styles of collegiate fun at their thirtieth reunion in 1970.

▼
One More Rutgers Lineage
Left to right: Carl Woodward, Jr., '40, microbiologist; Carl Woodward, Sr., '14, instructor at
the College of Agriculture, secretary to the president of Rutgers, and president of the University
of Rhode Island; and Carl Woodward III, '63,
now a lawyer—all in their respective class hats
in 1962.

Sources and Further Reading

This book is based on primary documents in the University Archives in Special Collections and Archives, Alexander Library, Rutgers University: alumni papers; student diaries, letters, scrapbooks, and broadsheets; faculty minutes; the *Targum*, the *Scarlet Letter*, and other student publications; the *Rutgers Alumni Magazine*; and of course on photographs and other illustrative materials. The most accurate and comprehensive secondary source on Rutgers history is Richard P. McCormick's *Rutgers: A Bicentennial History* (New Brunswick, 1966). On Rutgers in the 1960s, see Richard P. McCormick, "Rutgers, the State University," in David Riesman and Verne A. Stadtman, eds., *Academic Transformation* (New York, 1973). Other useful secondary sources include William H. S. Demarest's *History of Rutgers College, 1766–1924* (New Brunswick, 1924); George Lukac's *Aloud to Alma Mater* (New Brunswick, 1966); Jean Wilson Sidar's *George Hamell Cook: A Life in Agriculture and Geology, 1818–1889* (New Brunswick, 1976); and Francis Johns's "The Peithessophian Society Library Catalogue of 1834," *Journal of the Rutgers University Library* 44 (1982): 95–107. See also the eighty-nine sources listed in "Rutgers Reference Roundup: A Selective Bibliography of Materials Relating to the History of Rutgers University," finder's guide, Special Collections and Archives, compiled by Susan E. Avallone, June 1984.

For more general approaches to the history of American colleges and student life, see Lawrence R. Veysey's *The Emergence of the American University* (Chicago, 1965); and James McLachlan's critique of Veysey, "The American College in the Nineteenth Century: Toward a Reappraisal," *Teachers College Record*, December 1978. Good analyses of nineteenth-century American collegiate student culture are found in James McLachlan's "Choice of Hercules: American Student Societies in the Early Nineteenth Century," in *The University in Society*, edited by Lawrence Stone, volume 2 (Princeton, 1974); and in David F. Allmendinger, Jr.'s *Paupers and Scholars* (New York, 1975). Henry D. Sheldon's *American and European Student Culture, Nineteenth Century and Earlier* (New York, 1901) is a fascinating, if analytically primitive, catalog of pre-twentieth-century collegiate student culture.

Still more general—and highly informative—histories of American and western European youth from the eighteenth to the twentieth centuries are found in John Gillis's *Youth and History: Tradition and Change in European Age Relations, 1770–Present* (New York, 1981); and in Joseph F. Kett's *Rites of Passage: Adolescence in America, 1790 to the Present* (New York, 1977). Useful sociological studies of recent American student life include Walter L. Wallace's *Student Culture: Social Structure and Continuity in a Liberal Arts College* (Chicago, 1966); and Kenneth A. Feldman and Theodore M. Newcomb's *The Impact of College on Students* (San Francisco, 1969). For an ethnographically based study of student culture at contemporary Rutgers, see Michael Moffatt's "Student Culture: Participant-Observation in Rutgers College Residence Halls, 1977–1979," 1982, working paper deposited in Archives and Special Collections, Alexander Library; and *Youth Culture in an American College* (forthcoming).

All of the graphic materials in this book were taken from the primary and secondary sources in the Special Collections and Archives, Rutgers University Libraries, with the following exceptions:

Credits

Courtesy of The Agricultural Museum of the State of New Jersey:
Prints by Richard W. Mitchell from the original negatives in the George H. Cook Collection of Agricultural and Scientific Photographs—of an agricultural class (p. 47), Passion Puddle in 1901 (p. 122), the Agricultural School (p. 123), and agriculture students (pp. 124–125)

Courtesy of Susan E. Avallone:
Party invitation, Gamma Phi Beta Sorority (p. 244), scrapbook photographs (p. 245)

Courtesy of The Chicago Tribune:
Permission to reprint "The Nearsighted Mr. Magoo," © 1966, (255)

Courtesy of The Daily Targum:
Photographs of Lynch Bridge (p. 192), a toilet-paper fight (p. 225), and June Olkowski (p. 253)

Courtesy of William Gillam:
Photograph of freshmen at Hegeman (p. 158), poem from The Anthologist (p. 161), and photograph of members of the Class of 1940 (p. 258)

Courtesy of Martin Goldman:
Photograph of Dean Stayton Wood and staff (p. 201)

Courtesy of Louis Miller:
Scrapbook page (p. 223)

Courtesy of Thomas Rockwell, Norman Rockwell Estate:
Permission to reprint "Another Rugers Man—On The Way" by Norman Rockwell (p. 238)

Courtesy of Rutgers Alumni-Faculty Club:
Permission to photograph William M. Boyd's painting of the first football game (p. 75)

Courtesy of Rutgers Alumni Magazine:
Photographs of William Van Dyke (p. 77), a student theater production (p. 209), fraternity men (p. 209), a 1960 class schedule (p. 210), a parents' reception (p. 215), Richard Zabriskie (p. 216), and the Alpha Gamma Rho fraternity members (p. 227)

Courtesy of Rutgers News Service:
Permission to reproduce title page from 1770 Charter (p. 16); photographs of

Japanese students' graves (p. 49), the River Dorms (p. 183), Newark Campus (p. 189), the university planner (p. 190), University Heights Campus (p. 190), Dean Ernest Lynton (p. 191), President Mason Gross (p. 191), New Brunswick (p. 193), the three post-war presidents (pp. 194–195), Russell Kroeker (p. 228), the ROTC building (p. 230), a student demonstration (p. 230), and the bomb scare sign (p. 231)

Courtesy of Rutgers Sports Information:

Photographs of the Football Centennial (p. 248), Barbara Specht (p. 248), a football player (p. 249), the Rutgers-Virginia game (p. 250), the varsity football coaching staff, 1982 (p. 251), Dick Anderson (p. 251), the 1976 varsity basketball team (p. 252), Logg, Jr. and Price (p. 254), and Ed Trabulsy (p. 254)

Courtesy of Time, Inc:

Permission to reprint November 7, 1949 *Time* cover (p.164), © 1949 by Time, Inc. All rights reserved.

Courtesy of Universal Press Syndicate:

Permission to reprint "Doonesbury," (p.225), © 1972, by G. B. Trudeau

Courtesy of Carl R. Woodward Jr.:

Photographs by Mrs. Carl R. Woodward, Jr. (p. 153), and by James A. Stackhouse, Jr., Class of 1940, of Woodward Rutgers alumni (p. 259)

Courtesy of Parker Worley:

Photograph of Ayer building (p.188)

If you have comments on this volume or on any of the particular photographs in it, please let us know. In some cases, we could use help with the captions; many of the photos collected here have no identifying marks on them. In many cases, we *do* know the identities of persons shown. We would appreciate help with dates, or with the reasons or occasions for particular photos (examples: "Panorama of Rutgers Students, 1920s," pp. 126–127; "Queen's Players," pp. 142–143; the first photo in "Student Rooms," pp. 218–219—which almost looks like a stage set). Your comments may contribute to a future revision of *The Rutgers Picture Book*. Please send them to:

Michael Moffatt
c/o Rutgers University Press
30 College Avenue
New Brunswick, New Jersey 08903

Also, if looking through this volume reminds you of photos or documents that you have in your possession, please consider donating them to the University Archives in Special Collections and Archives. To discuss a donation, please contact:

Special Collections and Archives
Rutgers University Libraries
George and Huntington Streets
New Brunswick, New Jersey 08903

201–932–7006

Final Note to Loyal Sons and Daughters of Old Rutgers